Thomas James, bp. Conaty

New Testament Studies

The principal Events in the Life of our Lord

Thomas James, bp. Conaty

New Testament Studies
The principal Events in the Life of our Lord

ISBN/EAN: 9783743336438

Manufactured in Europe, USA, Canada, Australia, Japa

Cover: Foto ©Lupo / pixelio.de

Manufactured and distributed by brebook publishing software (www.brebook.com)

Thomas James, bp. Conaty

New Testament Studies

CONTENTS.

	PAGE
DEDICATION	5
INTRODUCTION	7
HINTS FOR THE CLASS-ROOM	10

PRELIMINARY STUDIES.

	PAGE		PAGE
Lesson I.	19	Lesson VI	22
Lesson II	20	Lesson VII	22
Lesson III	20	Lesson VIII	23
Lesson IV	21	Lesson IX	23
Lesson V	21	Lesson X	24

BIBLE TALKS: Why we should Love the Bible.... 24

Lesson XI	26	Lesson XIX	30
Lesson XII	27	Lesson XX	31
Lesson XIII	27	Lesson XXI	31
Lesson XIV	28	Lesson XXII	32
Lesson XV	28	Lesson XXIII	32
Lesson XVI	29	Lesson XXIV	33
Lesson XVII	29	Lesson XXV	33
Lesson XVIII	29	Lesson XXVI	34

BIBLE TALKS: Inspiration of the Bible........ 34

Lesson XXVII	36	Lesson XXIX	37
Lesson XXVIII	36	Lesson XXX	37

THE LIFE OF OUR BLESSED SAVIOUR.

PART I.

BEFORE BETHLEHEM.

IN THE BEGINNING WAS THE WORD.

Lesson XXXI	39	Lesson XXXIII	40
Lesson XXXII	39	Lesson XXXIV	40

BIRTH OF ST. JOHN THE BAPTIST FORETOLD.

	PAGE		PAGE
Lesson XXXV	42	Lesson XXXVIII	43
Lesson XXXVI	42	Lesson XXXIX	44
Lesson XXXVII	43		

BIBLE TALKS: The Temple at Jerusalem............ 44

THE ANNUNCIATION.

Lesson XL	45	Lesson XLII	47
Lesson XLI	46	Lesson XLIII	48

THE VISITATION.

Lesson XLIV	48	Lesson XLVI	50
Lesson XLV	50	Lesson XLVII	51

BIRTH OF ST. JOHN THE BAPTIST.

Lesson XLVIII	52	Lesson LI	54
Lesson XLIX	53	Lesson LII	55
Lesson L	54		

BIBLE TALKS: How to Interpret the Bible............ 56

PART II.

THE INFANCY OF CHRIST.

THE NATIVITY OF CHRIST.

Lesson LIII	58	Lesson LVI	60
Lesson LIV	59	Lesson LVII	61
Lesson LV	60		

THE PRESENTATION.

Lesson LVIII	62	Lesson LX	64
Lesson LIX	63	Lesson LXI	64

THE ADORATION OF THE MAGI.

	PAGE		PAGE
Lesson LXII	65	Lesson LXIV	67
Lesson LXIII	67	Lesson LXV	68
BIBLE TALKS: How to Interpret the Bible (continued)			69

THE FLIGHT INTO EGYPT.

Lesson LXVI	70	Lesson LXIX	73
Lesson LXVII	71	Lesson LXX	73
Lesson LXVIII	72		

PART III.

THE YOUTH OF CHRIST.

THE BOYHOOD OF CHRIST.

Lesson LXXI	75	Lesson LXXIII	77
Lesson LXXII	76	Lesson LXXIV	78
BIBLE TALKS: Bible Geography			78

JESUS IN THE TEMPLE.

Lesson LXXV	80	Lesson LXXVII	81
Lesson LXXVI	80	Lesson LXXVIII	82
BIBLE TALKS: Jewish Customs for Youth			83

PREACHING OF JOHN IN THE DESERT.

Lesson LXXIX	84	Lesson LXXXII	86
Lesson LXXX	85	Lesson LXXXIII	87
Lesson LXXXI	86		
BIBLE TALKS: Nazareth and the Education of the Jews			88

PART IV.

PREPARATION FOR PUBLIC LIFE.

THE BAPTISM OF JESUS IN THE JORDAN.

	PAGE		PAGE
Lesson LXXXIV	91	Lesson LXXXVI	92
Lesson LXXXV	91	Lesson LXXXVII	93

THE TEMPTATION OF JESUS.

Lesson LXXXVIII	93	Lesson XCI	96
Lesson LXXXIX	95	Lesson XCII	97
Lesson XC	95		

BIBLE TALKS: Journeys of Jesus 98

REVIEW.

Lesson XCIII	99	Lesson XCV	99
Lesson XCIV	99	Lesson XCVI	100

BIBLE TALKS: The Bible and Tradition 100

PART V.

THE PUBLIC LIFE OF CHRIST.

First Year of His Ministry.

ST. JOHN THE BAPTIST ANNOUNCES CHRIST.

Lesson XCVII	103	Lesson XCIX	104
Lesson XCVIII	104	Lesson C	105

THE MIRACLE AT CANA.

Lesson CI	106	Lesson CIV	109
Lesson CII	107	Lesson CV	109
Lesson CIII	108		

BIBLE TALKS: A Jewish Marriage **110**

JESUS AT CAPHARNAUM.

	PAGE		PAGE
Lesson CVI	111	Lesson CVIII	113
Lesson CVII	112	Lesson CIX	113
BIBLE TALKS: The Bible and Tradition (continued)			114

CHRIST PURGES THE TEMPLE.

Lesson CX	116	Lesson CXII	118
Lesson CXI	117	Lesson CXIII	118

JESUS AND NICODEMUS.

Lesson CXIV	119	Lesson CXVII	122
Lesson CXV	121	Lesson CXVIII	123
Lesson CXVI	121		

JESUS AND THE SAMARITAN WOMAN.

Lesson CXIX	124	Lesson CXXI	126
Lesson CXX	125	Lesson CXXII	127
BIBLE TALKS: The Catholic Church Loves the Bible			128

HEALING OF THE NOBLEMAN'S SON.

Lesson CXXIII	130	Lesson CXXV	132
Lesson CXXIV	131	Lesson CXXVI	133

JESUS AT NAZARETH.

Lesson CXXVII	134	Lesson CXXIX	136
Lesson CXXVIII	135	Lesson CXXX	137

Second Year of Christ's Ministry.

CHRIST'S FIRST DISCIPLES.

Lesson CXXXI	138	Lesson CXXXIV	141
Lesson CXXXII	139	Lesson CXXXV	141
Lesson CXXXIII	140		
BIBLE TALKS: The Catholic Church Preserved the Bible			142

THE CALL OF ST. MATTHEW.

	PAGE		PAGE
Lesson CXXXVI.........	145	Lesson CXXXVIII.......	146
Lesson CXXXVII........	145	Lesson CXXXIX.........	147
BIBLE TALKS. The Dead Sea............................			148

THE CALL OF THE TWELVE APOSTLES.

Lesson CXL.............	149	Lesson CXLII..........	151
Lesson CXLI............	150	Lesson CXLIII.........	151

THE SERMON ON THE MOUNT.

Lesson CXLIV..........	152	Lesson CXLVI..........	155
Lesson CXLV...........	154	Lesson CXLVII.........	156
BIBLE TALKS. The Bible and the People...................			156

Third Year of Christ's Ministry.

MULTIPLICATION OF THE LOAVES AND FISHES.

Lesson CXLVIII........	158	Lesson CL.............	161
Lesson CXLIX..........	160	Lesson CLI............	162

CHRIST PROMISES THE EUCHARIST.

Lesson CLII............	163	Lesson CLIV...........	165
Lesson CLIII...........	164	Lesson CLV............	166

PARABLES OF CHRIST.

Lesson CLVI...........	167	Lesson CLVIII.........	169
Lesson CLVII..........	168	Lesson CLIX...........	171
BIBLE TALKS. The Bible and the People (continued)........			171

Miracles of Christ.

1. *The Widow of Naim.*

Lesson CLX............	174	Lesson CLXI...........	175

2. The Ruler's Daughter.

	PAGE		PAGE
Lesson CLXII	176	Lesson CLXIII	177

THE TRANSFIGURATION.

Lesson CLXIV	178	Lesson CLXVI	181
Lesson CLXV	180	Lesson CLXVII	182

THE RAISING OF LAZARUS.

Lesson CLXVIII	183	Lesson CLXX	185
Lesson CLXIX	184	Lesson CLXXI	186
BIBLE TALKS. The Bible and the People (concluded)			187

THE RICH YOUNG MAN.

Lesson CLXXII	188	Lesson CLXXIV	191
Lesson CLXXIII	190	Lesson CLXXV	192

Holy Week.

THE TRIUMPHAL ENTRY INTO JERUSALEM.

Lesson CLXXVI	193	Lesson CLXXVIII	195
Lesson CLXXVII	194	Lesson CLXXIX	196

THE LAST SUPPER.

Lesson CLXXX	197	Lesson CLXXXII	199
Lesson CLXXXI	198	Lesson CLXXXIII	200

CHRIST AT GETHSEMANI.

Lesson CLXXXIV	201	Lesson CLXXXVI	204
Lesson CLXXXV	203	Lesson CLXXXVII	205
BIBLE TALKS: Douay College			206

The Day of the Passion.

THE BETRAYAL.

Lesson CLXXXVIII	207	Lesson CXC	209
Lesson CLXXXIX	208	Lesson CXCI	210

CHRIST BEFORE THE HIGH PRIEST.

	PAGE		PAGE
Lesson CXCII	212	Lesson CXCIV	214
Lesson CXCIII	213	Lesson CXCV	215

JESUS BEFORE PILATE.

Lesson CXCVI	216	Lesson CXCVIII	218
Lesson CXCVII	217	Lesson CXCIX	219

JESUS CONDEMNED TO DEATH.

Lesson CC	220	Lesson CCII	223
Lesson CCI	222	Lesson CCIII	224

THE CRUCIFIXION.

Lesson CCIV	225	Lesson CCVI	227
Lesson CCV	226	Lesson CCVII	228

The Days of Triumph.

THE RESURRECTION.

Lesson CCVIII	229	Lesson CCIX	231

THE WOMEN OF THE RESURRECTION.

Lesson CCX	232	Lesson CCXI	234

THE RISEN CHRIST WITH HIS APOSTLES.

Lesson CCXII... 235

PRIMACY OF ST. PETER.

Lesson CCXIII.. 236

THE ASCENSION.

Lesson CCXIV.. 239

Bible Dictionary... 241

NEW TESTAMENT STUDIES.

PRELIMINARY STUDIES.

LESSON I.

TEXT.—"And you shall give testimony, because you are with Me from the beginning." (John xv. 27.)

REFLECTION.—Mission of the apostles.

1. What is the Bible?
The Bible is the written word of God.

2. Into what parts is the Bible divided?
Into the Old and New Testaments.

3. What is meant by Testament?
Testament here means the record of the alliance or covenant of God with man.

4. What is meant by the Old Testament?
The record of the alliance or covenant of God with the Jews through Moses.

LESSON II.

Text.—"He that loveth Me not, keepeth not My words." (John xiv. 24.)

Reflection.—True Christian life.

5. What is meant by the New Testament?
The record of the alliance or covenant of God with the Christian people through Jesus Christ.

6. In what does the Bible differ from other books?
In this, that it alone is inspired by God.

7. What do you mean by inspiration?
I mean that God influences the mind of the writer, moving him to write, and so acting on him while he writes that his writing is the word of God.

8. Why did God do this?
One reason is in order to preserve accurately the record of God's dealings with men.

LESSON III.

Text.—"All power is given to Me in heaven and in earth; going therefore teach ye all nations." (Matt. xxviii. 18, 19.)

Reflection.—Authority of the Church.

9. Is the Bible, then, the word of God?
Yes, it is, because God inspired those who wrote it.

10. Can the Bible contain any errors?
It cannot, because it is the inspired word of God.

11. Can the Bible be opposed to science?
Certainly not, because science is but the knowledge of nature, and God is the author of nature as well as of the Bible.

12. Was the Bible written to teach science?
No, it was written to teach us principally what God has done for man, and what man must do for God.

LESSON IV.

TEXT.—"Go out into the highways and hedges: and compel them to come in, that My house may be filled." (Luke xiv. 23.)
REFLECTION.—The Eucharistic banquet.

13. Are there great scientists who make science agree with the Bible?
There certainly are many great men who hold that no scientific error is taught in the Bible.

14. Who wrote the first books of the Old Testament, and when?
Moses wrote the first five books, about 1500 years before Christ and 2500 years after Adam.

15. What is the authority for the books of the Bible?
In the Old Law, for the Jews it was the Jewish synagogue; and for us it is the Catholic Church, commissioned by Christ to teach all truth. The Church tells us which books are inspired and which form the Bible.

LESSON V.

TEXT.—"But one of the soldiers with a spear opened His side, and immediately there came out blood and water." (John xix. 34.)
REFLECTION.—Love of the Sacred Heart.

16. What does the word canon mean?
It is from the Greek and means rule or catalogue.

17. What is meant by canon of Scripture, or sacred canon?
It means the list or catalogue of sacred books which are declared by competent authority to be the rule or standard of faith and morals.

18. Is it the only standard of life?

By no means, as those books do not contain all that is to be believed or done.

LESSON VI.

Text.—"Ask: and it shall be given you: seek, and you shall find; knock, and it shall be opened to you." (Luke xi. 9.)

Reflection.—Power of prayer.

19. Into how many classes do you divide the books of Scripture?

Into proto-canonical and deutero-canonical books.

20. What do you mean by proto-canonical books?

Those books which were accepted as sacred and canonical from the beginning.

21. What is meant by deutero-canonical?

Those books about the sacred character of which some doubt for a while existed.

LESSON VII.

Text.—"Master, we have labored all the night, and have taken nothing." (Luke v. 5.)

Reflection.—Faith in God.

22. When were the first books of the Bible gathered together in one volume?

Probably in the days of Josue, about 1400 years before Christ.

23. What books did it contain?

It contained the Pentateuch, or five Books of Moses, to which was added the Book of Josue.

24. When was the Jewish canon completed, and by whom?

Before the coming of Christ, and by the synagogue.

LESSON VIII.

TEXT.—"If therefore thou offer thy gift at the altar, and there thou remember that thy brother hath anything against thee, leave there thy offering before the altar and go first to be reconciled to thy brother." (Matt. v. 23, 24.)

REFLECTION.—Forgiveness.

25. Who was the writer of the first books of the Old Testament?

Moses, who wrote the Pentateuch, consisting of Genesis, Exodus, Leviticus, Numbers, and Deuteronomy.

26. From what sources did Moses draw for the Book of Genesis?

From the oral traditions of the patriarchs and prophets for 2500 years.

27. In what languages was the Old Testament written?

Hebrew, Chaldaic, and Greek.

LESSON IX.

TEXT.—"Because every one that exalteth himself, shall be humbled: and he that humbleth himself, shall be exalted." (Luke xiv. 11.)

REFLECTION.—The glory of humility.

28. Name some other writers of the Old Testament books.

Josue, Samuel, David, Solomon, Isaias, and Jeremias.

29. When was the first version of the Old Testament made?

It was begun about three hundred years before Christ.

30. What is it called, and in what language was it made?

It is called the Septuagint, and was written in Greek.

LESSON X.

TEXT.—"And the angel being come in said unto her [Mary]: Hail, full of grace, the Lord is with thee." (Luke i. 28.)

REFLECTION.—The power of Mary's name.

31. Whence did the Septuagint derive its name?

Septuagint means seventy, and is said to come from the tradition that seventy-two translators, six from each of the twelve tribes, were sent from Jerusalem to Alexandria at the request of Ptolemy to translate the Pentateuch.

32. Did Christ recognize the Jewish canons?

Yes, and all the apostles likewise.

33. How many books in the Old Testament?

As defined by the Council of Trent, there are forty-five.

BIBLE TALKS.

Why we should love the Bible.

In placing before you a method for the study of the New Testament we hope to help you gather for your instruction some of the beauties of the best book ever offered to man for his reading. No pearls so precious, no flowers so fragrant, no thoughts so beautiful. In all literature there is no history so eventful, no poetry so rich in imagery, no deeds of warriors so deserving of imitation and praise. It is the story of Our Redeemer, it is the poetry of a God's love, it is the record of a God who died for us on a cross that we might have heaven. That we may intelligently study our New Testament, it is necessary to recall what the Bible itself is, for we must remember that the New Testament is but the second part of the great book called the Bible.

What is the Bible? A book with history, prophecy, and moral teachings; a book which millions of intelligent beings look upon with respect and reverence, the teachings of which are accepted as facts, and the commandments of which are followed with conscientious fidelity. The Bible is not like other books, no matter how good they may be, nor how well written. It is the only book of its kind; it is the greatest of all books, because it alone is the written word of God. Men have written great books. Homer wrote the story of the Greeks, and his books come to us with all the beauty of style and all the sweet unction of a great poet, but at best they embody only the thought of Homer. Kempis has given us life thoughts which men read and love, because they are of the soul and lift us up to a taste of heavenly things, until the "Imitation" takes the character of something almost beyond the human, but the "Imitation" is Kempis's thought, and it is purely human; but the Bible is beyond the best and purest and most soul-inspiring of all things written, because the Bible is not the thought of man, but of God—the Bible is the word of God. Of all books written, the Bible is the only one inspired, and the inspiration of the Bible is from God and makes God the very author of what it contains. This is why it has been called God under the letter, almost as Christ dwells under the appearance of the bread of the sacrament. The Word made flesh dwelling on our altars—the Word made flesh speaking and living under the letters of the Book. What a treasure the Bible is! How man should reverence it! How men in every age have reverenced it! The Jews listened with uncovered heads, and in the solemnity of the Temple, to its reading. The Christians in their churches and homes kissed the sacred page, and on bended knees read its story. The Christian councils placed it on a throne of gold, while lighted tapers attested that it was life for the human mind and heart. As of old the ark of the covenant was sacred, because it contained the tablets of stone; so the Bible is sacred because it contains what was written by the inspired author, what God did for mankind in the Old Law, and what Christ and His apostles did in the New Law. Our Bible, then, is a sacred book, which we should reverence. It should not be looked upon as a school-book, but a holy thing, to be touched with devotion and to be read with piety. God speaks to us from its pages, and we should read it as if God's voice was speaking to us.

PRELIMINARY STUDIES (Continued).

LESSON XI.

Text.—"There stood by the cross of Jesus, His mother and His mother's sister, Mary of Cleophas, and Mary Magdalene." (John xix. 25.)

Reflection.—Compassion of the Blessed Virgin.

34. How many books in the New Testament?
According to the Council of Trent, there are twenty-seven.

35. Into what classes are they divided?
Historical, doctrinal, and prophetical, including the Gospels, Acts of the Apostles, the Epistles, and the Apocalypse.

36. Who were the authors of the New Testament?
Most probably the apostles and disciples whose names

are attached to their writings. St. Luke wrote the Acts and St. John the Apocalypse.

LESSON XII.

TEXT.—"Friend, how camest thou in hither not having on a wedding garment?" (Matt. xxii. 12.)

REFLECTION.—The wedding garment of divine grace.

37. In what languages was the New Testament written?

All was written in Greek except St. Matthew's gospel, which is generally supposed to have been first written in Hebrew.

38. When was the canon of Scripture first defined by the Christian Church?

In the Council of Hippo, in 393.

39. What Council settled definitely the canon, as we now receive it?

The Council of Trent, in the session of April 8, 1546.

LESSON XIII.

TEXT.—"Jesus saith to him: Go thy way, thy son liveth. The man believed the word which Jesus said to him and went his way." (John iv. 50.)

REFLECTION.—The power of faith.

40. What do you mean by versions of the Testament?

Translations into the many different languages.

41. Which was the first version in which we are specially interested, and when was it made?

The one in Latin, known as the Itala, because used by the Italian churches. It appeared in the first centuries, and is thought by some to have been made in Africa.

42. What is meant by the Latin Vulgate?

The Vulgate means *current text*, and is in part the old Itala revised by St. Jerome, and in part a new translation made by him.

LESSON XIV.

TEXT.—"So also shall My heavenly Father do to you, if you forgive not every one his brother from your hearts." (Matt. xviii. 35.)

REFLECTION.—Forgiveness.

43. Who induced St. Jerome to do this work?
Pope Damasus, who was governing the Catholic Church.

44. What authority has the Vulgate?
It is the authorized version used by the Catholic Church in all the liturgies of the Latin rite.

45. What is the version called which is used in the English by Catholics?
It is commonly called the Douay Bible. Part of it was translated at Rheims in 1582, and part of it at Douay in 1609.

LESSON XV.

TEXT.—"Render therefore to Cæsar the things that are Cæsar's; and to God, the things that are God's." (Matt. xxii. 21.)

REFLECTION.—Obedience to authority.

46. When was this version revised and adopted?
It was revised by Bishop Challoner of England in 1750, reprinted in Philadelphia in 1790 and adopted by our American bishops first in 1810 and again in 1837.

47. Which are the two divisions of the New Testament?
(1) The Holy Gospel, and Epistles; (2) the other inspired writings of the apostles and disciples, namely the Acts and the Apocalypse.

48. What is meant by the word gospel, and what does it contain?
It means *good tidings* or good message, and contains the life and words of Christ.

LESSON XVI.

Text.—"Be of good heart, daughter, thy faith hath made thee whole." (Matt. ix. 22.)

Reflection.—Confidence in God.

49. Are there not four gospels?
There is but one Gospel, but there are four records, by writers who give the history of Christ as it appeared to them.

50. Did each writer have a special object in writing his gospel?
Yes, it appears in the reason for which each one wrote.

51. Who were the Evangelists?
Matthew and John, who were apostles; Mark and Luke, who were disciples.

LESSON XVII.

Text.—"Go, shew thyself to the priest, and offer the gift which Moses commanded for a testimony unto them." (Matt. viii. 4.)

Reflection.—Foreshadowing of Confession.

52. For whom did St. Matthew write?
He wrote his gospel especially for the converted Jews.

53. What object had he in writing his gospel?
His object was to show that Christ was the Messias whom they expected.

54. What is this gospel sometimes called?
The gospel of the humanity of Christ.

LESSON XVIII.

Text.—"What manner of man is this, for the winds and the sea obey Him?" (Matt. viii. 27.)

Reflection.—Confidence in God.

55. Why is St. Matthew's gospel called the gospel of the humanity of Christ?
Because not only does it open with the human genealogy

of Christ, and show His descent from Adam, but also because it proves that He is the one foretold by the prophets to the Hebrews.

56. Who was St. Matthew?

He was a Galilean by birth, a tax-gatherer or publican by occupation, near Lake Genesareth, until Christ called him to be an apostle. He preached the Gospel in the East, and died for the faith.

57. When, where, and in what language was his gospel written?

It was generally believed to have been written about thirteen or fourteen years after the Ascension; it was written in Palestine, and originally in Hebrew or Aramaic. It was soon translated into Greek, some say, by St. Matthew himself. This translation alone remains.

LESSON XIX.

TEXT.—"Gather up first the cockle, and bind it into bundles to burn, but the wheat gather ye into my barn." (Matt. xiii. 30.)
REFLECTION.—The harvest-day at the Last Judgment.

58. Who was St. Mark?

He is thought to have been a Jew converted by St. Peter and made his interpreter. Mark was his Latin surname, his Jewish name being John, so that he was called "John whose surname was Mark."

59. What object had he in writing?

To show to the Gentiles, and especially the Romans, the goodness and mercy and love of Jesus Christ, as preached by St. Peter.

60. Where and when was it written?

It is commonly believed to have been written in Rome, during the lifetime of St. Peter, probably between A.D. 63 and A.D. 70.

LESSON XX.

TEXT.—"The kingdom of heaven is like to a grain of mustard-seed, which a man took and sowed in his field." (Matt. xiii. 31.)

REFLECTION.—The Catholic Church, the mustard-seed.

61. What is St. Mark's gospel sometimes called, and why?

The gospel of St. Peter, because it is a record of St. Peter's teaching, and was written under his eye and direction.

62. In what language was it written?

In Greek, which was much used at that time by the Church at Rome, and also in the Churches of the West.

63. In what city did St. Mark preach?

After the death of St. Peter, St. Mark visited Egypt, and founded the Church of Alexandria. His principal preaching was done in Alexandria.

LESSON XXI.

TEXT.—"For as lightning cometh out of the East, and appeareth even into the West: so shall also the coming of the Son of man be." (Matt. xxiv. 27.)

REFLECTION.—The Last Judgment Day.

64. Who was St. Luke?

He was a native of Antioch, a physician by profession, a convert from the Gentiles, and a disciple of St. Paul.

65. For whom did he write his gospel?

For those who, like himself, were converted from paganism. It is sometimes called the Gospel of the Greeks.

66. What is the object of his gospel?

To show the priestly office of Jesus Christ, and to record some of His conversations.

LESSON XXII.

Text.—"And then they shall see the Son of man coming in a cloud with great power and majesty." (Luke xxi. 27.)

Reflection.—The Last Judgment.

67. Why did St. Luke write his gospel?
To prove that Christ was the Redeemer of all men.

68. To whom was it specially addressed?
To Theophilus, who is supposed to have been a distinguished man, one of St. Luke's converts. It seems to have been written especially for the Gentile converts, to whom this man belonged.

69. When and where was this gospel written?
Either at Cesarea, A.D. 56–58, or at Rome, A.D. 62–66, probably while St. Paul was in prison. Some say that it was not published until after St. Paul's death.

LESSON XXIII.

Text.—"The blind see, the lame walk, the lepers are cleansed, the deaf hear, the dead rise again, the poor have the Gospel preached to them." (Matt. xi. 5.)

Reflection.—The works of Jesus Christ.

70. In what language was St. Luke's gospel written?
In Greek, with a style so polished as to make it the most classical of all the gospels.

71. What is this gospel sometimes called?
The gospel of consolation.

72. Why is it so called?
Because it shows the mercy of Christ for all men, Jew and Gentile, and especially for the poor and despised.

LESSON XXIV.

TEXT.—"He [John] said: I am the voice of one crying in the wilderness: make straight the way of the Lord, as said the prophet Isaias." (John i. 23.)

REFLECTION.—Preparation for the coming of Christ.

73. Who was St. John?

He was the brother of James and son of Zebedee, who was a fisherman of Galilee.

74. What is he frequently called?

"The beloved disciple," "the disciple whom Jesus loved."

75. Why did St. John write his gospel?

That he might show the divinity of Christ, as also to complete the history as told by the other Evangelists.

LESSON XXV.

TEXT.—"Prepare ye the way of the Lord: make straight His paths. And all flesh shall see the salvation of God." (Luke iii. 4, 6.)

REFLECTION.—The necessity of penance.

76. How does St. John himself express the reason for his writing?

"These [things] have been written that ye may believe that Jesus is the Christ, the Son of God, and that believing, ye may have life in His name." (John xx. 31.)

77. Where and when was this gospel written?

Most probably in Ephesus, and late in the apostle's life, some time after A.D. 80.

78. In what language was it written?

It was written in Greek, but it has many Hebrew expressions.

LESSON XXVI.

Text.—"And thy own soul a sword shall pierce, that out of many hearts thoughts may be revealed." (Luke ii. 35.)

Reflection.—Joy mingled with sorrow.

79. What is this gospel sometimes called?

The gospel of eternity, because it describes the eternal generation of Christ. It is also called the "gospel of love."

80. What relation do the first three gospels hold to the fourth?

They lead us to see in Jesus Christ the perfect Son of man, while St. John shows us Jesus Christ as the perfect Son of God.

81. For whom, then, may we say St. John's gospel was written?

For Jew and Gentile; that the Jew may believe that Jesus is the Messias, and that the Gentile may see that the same Jesus is the Son of God, and thus both may be united in faith and be saved.

BIBLE TALKS.

Inspiration of the Bible.

We have seen the great value and beauty of the Bible, and we honor and reverence it as the best of all books, because it alone is the inspired word of God. Now let us understand what is meant when we call it the inspired word of God. What is inspiration? Inspiration is from the Latin, and means a breathing into. In relation to the Scriptures it means that God, as it were, breathed into the minds of the writers and assisted them to write the truth, and protected them from all falsehood. This was a grace of God bestowed upon the writers of the sacred books, and belonged to the writers only for the work of writing the sacred records. When their books were written, the inspiration ceased.

According to the Church teaching, inspiration really consisted of two graces, one for the intellect and the other for the will. For example, when Moses wrote his books, or St. Matthew his gospel, God enlightened their minds with the knowledge of what they were to write, and He also moved their wills to write it. Thus it was not merely a message from God to men, nor a record of God's deeds or words, but the very word of God, and that word written by God through the agency of these writers. Hence, inspiration means that God is the agent inspiring, while the inspired writer is the instrument God uses, but this instrument is intelligent, free, and voluntary. In this way the inspired writers retained all their characteristics as writers, and their style was their own. Hear how the learned St. Jerome expresses it: "Isaias the prophet had the style of a nobleman and the eloquence of the city, while Jeremias the prophet had the rustic style of the villager of Anathoth, but the truths were equal as prophesied by the Spirit." It is the original manuscript, the autographic copy, that is inspired. The copies of the original and the translations are inspired only inasmuch as they are conformable to the original autographic copy. The translation is called authentic or without error, and has to be approved, by the Church, in order to be accepted. Among the Jews before Christ, the canon of Scripture, or the books used by the synagogue, as the teaching tribunal was called, were received as inspired, and Our Saviour and the apostles quoted from them as the word of God.

Several of the great Councils of the Church teach us the inspiration of the Sacred Scriptures, and we find that the Vatican Council, held in 1870, repeats what all the others had said in their words about the Bible: "These books the Church holds sacred because they were written by the *inspiration* of the Holy Ghost and have *God for their author.*" Now you understand what is meant by the inspiration of the Bible. You can see, therefore, what a holy book the Bible is, and why we reverence it as the word of God.

LESSON XXVII.

Text.—" For we have seen His star in the East, and are come to adore Him." (Matt. ii. 2.)

Reflection.—Faith of the wise men.

82. Did any of the prophecies of the Old Testament refer to the Evangelists?

Yes; it is supposed that in the first chapter of Ezechiel they were prefigured by the four cherubim.

83. To whom did these cherubim appear?

To the prophet Ezechiel, in a vision. See Ezechiel, chap. 1.

84. In what form did they appear?

With the face of a man, a lion, an ox, and an eagle.

LESSON XXVIII.

Text.—" And when he was twelve years old, they going into Jerusalem according to the custom of the feast, and having fulfilled the days, when they returned, the child Jesus remained in Jerusalem." (Luke ii. 42, 43.)

Reflection.—Fidelity to Church laws.

85. How is this vision explained?

According to St. Jerome, the man refers to St. Matthew, the lion to St. Mark, the ox to St. Luke, the eagle to St. John.

86. Do you find this in the character of their gospels?

Yes. St. Matthew deals with the humanity of Christ; St. Mark with His royalty; St. Luke with His priesthood; and St. John with His divinity.

87. How do you find the royalty in the lion?

The lion is the king of all beasts, and St. Mark opens his gospel with the roaring of the lion of penance, the great St. John the Baptist.

LESSON XXIX.

TEXT.—"His mother saith to the waiters: Whatsoever He shall say to you, do ye." (John ii. 5.)

REFLECTION.—Influence of Mary with Jesus.

88. How do you find the priesthood prefigured in the ox?

By the sacrifices of the Jewish priesthood, with which St. Luke opens his gospel.

89. Are these figures used as emblems of the Evangelists?

Yes, Christian art has so consecrated them.

90. Who tells us that this is the correct meaning of the figures?

It is largely based upon the commentaries of the Fathers who explain them to us.

LESSON XXX.

TEXT.—"And behold a leper came and adored Him, saying: Lord, if Thou wilt, Thou canst make me clean." (Matt. viii. 2.)

REFLECTION.—The leprosy of sin.

91. What are the gospels of St. Matthew, St. Mark, and St. Luke, when taken together, sometimes called?

They are called the synoptic gospels because, when arranged in sections of parallel columns, they give a general view of Our Lord's life and teachings.

92. What is the gospel of St. John called in relation to these?

It is called the supplementary or doctrinal gospel.

93. On what do we rely for the true sense of the Bible?

Upon the decrees of the Church and interpretations of the Fathers, who in all ages have expressed the sense of the Church, which has been authorized by Christ to teach mankind.

THE LIFE OF OUR BLESSED SAVIOUR.

PART I.

Before Bethlehem.

"In the Beginning was the Word."

Read carefully and memorize verses 1-14 of the First Chapter of St. John's gospel.

LESSON XXXI.

TEXT.—"And His disciples came to Him, and awaked Him, saying: Lord, save us, we perish." (Matt. viii. 25.)
REFLECTION.—How near God is to us always.

94. In studying the life of Christ what is the first element to be considered?
That Christ is the Son of God, existing from all eternity, and having the very nature of God; in fact, that He is God.

95. Where do we find this taught in the Gospel?
In the gospel of St. John, chap. i., verses 1 to 5.

96. Will you repeat the words of the Gospel?
1. "In the beginning was the Word, and the Word was with God, and the Word was God.
2. "The same was in the beginning with God.
3. "All things were made by Him: and without Him was made nothing that was made.
4. "In Him was life, and the life was the light of men:
5. "And the light shineth in darkness, and the darkness did not comprehend it."

LESSON XXXII.

TEXT.—"Call the laborers and pay them their hire, beginning from the last even to the first." (Matt. xx. 8.)
REFLECTION.—God's reward for service.

97. What does the Evangelist mean by those words "In the beginning"?
He wishes to express the idea that Christ existed before the creation of the world or anything else that was created.

98. What does he mean by the "Word"?
He thus names the Second Person of the Blessed Trinity,

the Son of God, who is the Word of the Father, who thus reveals Himself.

99. Can you give some indication of this in human speech?

The word we utter is the expression of our thought. Christ is the expression of the thought of God, the Father.

LESSON XXXIII.

TEXT.—"And other some fell among thorns, and the thorns growing up with it, choked it." (Luke viii. 7.)

REFLECTION.—God's grace choked by human passions.

100. Why does he say "the Word was God"?

Because, being of the same nature as the Father, Christ is God like unto Him, distinct from Him, but equal to Him.

101. Does what follows explain this more fully?

Yes. He tells that all things were created by Him, and that He is "Light" and "Life," all of which can be said of no one but God.

102. What does he mean by calling His "Life" the "Light" of the world?

He means that He is the true light to illumine the world and show men the truth of God.

LESSON XXXIV.

TEXT.—"What wilt thou that I do to thee? But he said: Lord, that I may see." (Luke xviii. 41.)

REFLECTION.—The blindness of sin.

103. How does St. John express the coming of Christ to redeem mankind?

"And the Word was made flesh and dwelt among us." (John i. 14.)

104. What fact is here narrated?

The historical fact that the Word came into the world, manifesting Himself in the form of a man with flesh and blood like ours.

105. What do those words prove?

That the Son of God did not merely assume a body, but that He became man, and by the Incarnation God and man exist in one person, and that person is Jesus Christ, whose life we are studying.

Birth of St. John the Baptist Foretold.

Read carefully and study closely verses 5-25 of the First Chapter of St. Luke.
Read about the Temple of Jerusalem.

LESSON XXXV.

TEXT.—"And they were both just before God, walking in all the commandments and justifications of the Lord without blame." (Luke i. 6.)

REFLECTION.—Good people in a wicked world.

106. Which Herod is referred to in this first chapter of St. Luke?

Herod the Great, who slew the holy innocents. He was king of Judea, a Jew in religion, but an Idumean in race. It was his son who put John the Baptist to death and mocked Christ.

107. What was Zachary's relation to the Temple?

He was a priest of the Course of Abia, who was the chief priest of the Course.

108. What is meant by the Course of Abia?

The priesthood was divided into twenty-four Courses or Classes, to which was entrusted the care of sacred worship. Abia was the head of the Eighth Course.

LESSON XXXVI.

TEXT.—"But the angel said to him: Fear not, Zachary, for thy prayer is heard; and thy wife Elizabeth shall bear thee a son and thou shalt call his name John." (Luke i. 13.)

REFLECTION.—Power of prayer.

109. To what tribe did these two holy persons belong?

To the tribe of Levi and the family of Aaron, and hence were of priestly rank as well as of the Jewish nobility.

110. What was the priest's office?

To offer sacrifice in the Temple, to burn incense at the altar, to care for the lamps, and to renew the showbread.

111. What Temple is here referred to?
The Temple of Jerusalem, built, in great magnificence, by Herod the Great.

LESSON XXXVII.

TEXT.—"For he shall be great before the Lord; and shall drink no wine nor strong drink, and he shall be filled with the Holy Ghost even from his mother's womb." (Luke i. 15.)

REFLECTION.—The virtues of St. John the Baptist.

112. How many principal parts had the Temple?
Three parts: the Entrance-hall, the Holy Place, and the Holy of holies.

113. Where was Zachary when the angel appeared?
Near the golden altar of incense, which stood within the Holy Place; back of the altar was the veil which marked the Holy of holies.

114. Was a priest called frequently to minister at the altar of incense?
No, not more than twice in his life, because he had to take his turn, which came seldom to each one of twenty thousand priests.

LESSON XXXVIII.

TEXT.—"And the angel answering, said to him: I am Gabriel, who stand before God; and am sent to speak to thee, and to bring thee these good tidings." (Luke i. 19.)

REFLECTION.—Mission of the angels.

115. What hours were prescribed for the burning of incense at the golden altar?
At nine in the morning and three in the afternoon.

116. What peculiar dress was worn by the priest at this ceremony?
He wore white robes and, with unsandalled feet, stood ready to burn the incense as soon as the holocaust was offered at the great altar in the court.

117. What did the angel foretell to Zachary?

The birth of a son who would be great, because he was destined to go before the Saviour and thus be the Precursor or Forerunner.

LESSON XXXIX.

TEXT.—"And when he came out he could not speak to them, and they understood that he had seen a vision in the Temple. And he made signs to them, and remained dumb." (Luke i. 22.)

REFLECTION.—Punishment for unbelief.

118. How did Zachary receive the promise, and what was his punishment?

He doubted the word of the angel because of his own extreme age, and he was stricken with dumbness as a punishment and a confirmation of the promise.

119. How did Elizabeth receive the word?

With joy and happiness, because, like all Jewish women, she hoped to be the mother of the Redeemer.

120. What name was to be given to this child?

John was the name given by the angel Gabriel. He was afterwards to be known as the Baptist, because he baptized.

BIBLE TALKS.

The Temple at Jerusalem.

The great King David proposed to replace the Tabernacle and build a temple which would be worthy of the Jewish nation. His son Solomon was destined to perform this work, and he built a magnificent temple in Jerusalem, which was the pride and glory of all Hebrews. There were three temples, one succeeding the other. The first, beautifully pictured in 2 Paralipomenon, chap. iii., was called the temple of Solomon and was dedicated B.C. 1004, four hundred and eighty-six years after the dedication of the Tabernacle. It was destroyed by Nabuchodonosor. The second was the temple of Zorobabel and was dedicated four hundred and eighty-nine years after Solomon's, in the year

515 B.C. This is described in 1 Esdras vi. 3. The third was the temple of Herod, built four hundred and ninety-seven years later, from the remains of Zorobabel's, in the year 18 B.C. It lasted eighty-eight years and was destroyed under Titus, when Jerusalem was captured. Solomon's temple was the richest. It was built on the same plan as the Tabernacle, but it was twice its size. It was finished in carved cedar, fir, olive, and gold. Large courts surrounded the building, one for the priests and one for the people.

The third temple, which was the one spoken of in our lesson, was a magnificent structure. Years were given to complete the work. Josephus, the Jewish historian, says of it: "To strangers, who were approaching, it appeared at a distance like a mountain covered with snow; for where it was not decorated with plates of gold it was extremely white and glistening." From this temple Christ drove the buyers and sellers.

The Annunciation.

Read carefully and study verses 26–40 of the First Chapter of St. Luke.

LESSON XI.

TEXT.—" And in the sixth month, the angel Gabriel was sent from God into a city of Galilee, called Nazareth, To a virgin espoused to a man whose name was Joseph, of the house of David: and the virgin's name was Mary." (Luke i. 26, 27.)

REFLECTION.—The mission of the angels.

121. What is meant by the sixth month?

It means that six months had elapsed from the visit of the angel to Zachary until his visit to the Blessed Virgin at Nazareth.

122. Had Galilee been mentioned by any of the great prophets in connection with Our Saviour?

Yes, in Isaias ix. 1, 2, where it is spoken of as the scene of Christ's labors by which light comes to the people in darkness.

123. What can you tell us of Galilee?

Galilee was one of the four great Roman divisions of Palestine, north of Judea and Samaria, west of Perea, and

comprised the territories of Zabulon, Nephthali, Issachar, and Asher. It was rich and populous, and had many large towns.

LESSON XLI.

TEXT.—"And the angel being come in, said unto her: Hail full of grace: the Lord is with thee: Blessed art thou among women." (Luke i. 28.)

REFLECTION.—The virtues of our blessed Mother.

124. What do we know of Nazareth?

It was a secluded and obscure village of Galilee, lying in a narrow cleft of the hills, which formed the boundary of the territory of Zabulon to the north of the plain of Esdrelon.

125. Who is the Mary spoken of by St. Luke?
She is the virgin, betrothed to Joseph, and is the daughter of Joachim and Anna, and like Joseph belonged to the royal family of David. At three years of age, in the Temple, she consecrated her life to virginity.

126. Had this virgin been spoken of by the prophets?
Yes; Isaias, in the famous prophecy, chap. vii., v. 14, says: "Behold a virgin shall conceive, and bear a son, and his name shall be called Emmanuel." The Catholic Church teaches us that this refers to the Virgin Mary, Mother of Christ.

LESSON XLII.

TEXT.—" And the angel said to her: Fear not, Mary, for thou hast found grace with God." (Luke i. 30.)
REFLECTION.—God's reward for virtue.

127. What do you know of Joseph spoken of in the Gospel?
He was the son of Heli, and he was of the house and lineage of David. He was betrothed to the Blessed Virgin shortly before the Annunciation, and was a just man, who by his labor supported Mary and Jesus in Nazareth.

128. What was meant by the salutation of the angel?
It meant that Mary had received the fulness of sanctifying grace, and that there was no sin in her who was "blessed among women" and with whom "the Lord is."

129. Why was Mary troubled at the words of the angel?
Zachary was troubled at the very sight of the angel, but Mary was troubled at his words, and she wondered what they could mean, and whether the message was really from

God. She thought of her vow, and wondered how the message of the angel could be reconciled with it.

LESSON XLIII.

TEXT.—"Behold thou shalt conceive in thy womb, and shalt bring forth a Son, and thou shalt call His name Jesus." (Luke i. 31.)

REFLECTION.—Jesus our Saviour.

130. How did the angel receive her questions?

He answered by explaining to her how the Holy Spirit would effect the mystery of the Incarnation and that, while remaining a virgin, she would be blessed with the motherhood of Christ.

131. How did Mary receive this explanation?

In obedience to the will of God she acknowledged herself His handmaid, ready to accept the mission assigned to her.

132. What happened then?

Immediately, by the power of the Holy Ghost, our divine Saviour became incarnate, the Word was made flesh, and the mystery of the Incarnation took place.

The Visitation.

Read carefully and study verses 40-56 of the First Chapter of St. Luke's gospel, and especially the "Magnificat," verses 46-55.

LESSON XLIV.

TEXT.—"And Mary rising up in those days, went unto the hill country with haste, into a city of Juda: And she entered into the house of Zachary, and saluted Elizabeth." (Luke i. 39, 40.)

REFLECTION.—The charity of the Blessed Virgin.

THE VISITATION.

133. How soon after the Annunciation did the Blessed Virgin visit Elizabeth?

The words "In those days" would lead us to infer that it was very soon, and it is generally supposed to have been shortly afterwards.

134. Why did Mary make this visit?

That she might see the fulfilment of the angel's prophecy, rejoice with her cousin St. Elizabeth, and by the pres-

ence of Our Saviour, sanctify John the Baptist before his birth, and thus prepare him for his work, as forerunner of the redemption.

135. What is meant by the "hill country"?

Palestine, west of the Jordan, had one portion formed by a mass of low rounded hills which comprised most of the Roman provinces of Samaria and Judea. This was called the "hill country."

LESSON XLV.

Text.—"And Elizabeth was filled with the Holy Ghost. And she cried out with a loud voice: Blessed art thou among women, and blessed is the fruit of thy womb. And whence is this to me, that the Mother of my Lord should come to me?" (Luke i. 42, 43.)

Reflection.—The great dignity of the Mother of Jesus.

136. What city of Juda is referred to in the preceding lesson?

Some think it was Hebron; others that it was a small village where Zachary lived, about six miles west of Jerusalem, about seventy or eighty miles from Nazareth, and known as "St. John in the Mountain." The journey must have taken three or four days.

137. What time in the year was this journey?

It is generally believed to have been in the latter part of April, as the Annunciation of the angel occurred on March 25th.

138. How did Elizabeth receive her?

With joy and humility; and inspired by God she cried out: "Blessed art thou among women, and blessed is the fruit of thy womb." Then she saluted her as the Mother of God, exclaiming: "Whence is this to me, that the Mother of my Lord should come to me?"

LESSON XLVI.

Text.—"And Mary said: My soul doth magnify the Lord: And my spirit hath rejoiced in God my Saviour. Because He hath regarded the humility of His handmaid: for behold from henceforth all generations shall call me blessed." (Luke i. 46-48.)

Reflection.—Why we honor the Blessed Virgin.

139. How did Mary receive the praises of St. Elizabeth?

With a humility which came from a sense of her own unworthiness and God's great goodness to her.

THE VISITATION.

140. How did she express herself?

Inspired by God, she sang the beautiful canticle of the "Magnificat." It is so called because in the Latin the first word is "Magnificat," or "doth magnify."

141. What do we find in this canticle?

Intense religious fervor, intellectual force, and a most charming simplicity, which show the beauty and nobility of the character of Mary.

LESSON XLVII.

TEXT.—"He hath put down the mighty from their seat, and hath exalted the humble. He hath filled the hungry with good things: and the rich He hath sent empty away." (Luke i. 52, 53.)

REFLECTION.—Reward of humility.

142. How may the "Magnificat" be divided and analyzed?

It may be divided into four parts:

1. Personal gratitude for favors bestowed upon herself. (Luke i. 46-48.)
2. Praise of God's power and mercy. (Luke i. 49, 50.)
3. Humility rewarded and pride punished. (Luke i. 51-53.)
4. God's faithfulness to all His promises. (Luke i. 54, 55.)

143. Are there hymns in the Old Testament somewhat resembling the "Magnificat," and would Mary be likely to know them?

Yes; the hymn of Judith (Judith xvi. 1-17), and that of Anna the mother of Samuel (1 Kings ii. 1-10), but especially the latter. Every Hebrew child was taught these and other hymns, and sang them at the feasts in Jerusalem.

144. How long did Mary remain with St. Elizabeth?

The Gospel says that "Mary abode with her about three months." Some think she remained until after the birth of John the Baptist.

Birth of St. John the Baptist.

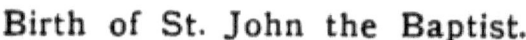

Read carefully and study verses 57-80 of the First Chapter of St. Luke's gospel. Compare them with verses 6, 7, 8, and 15-36 of the First Chapter of St. John's gospel.

LESSON XLVIII.

TEXT.—"And it came to pass that on the eighth day they came to circumcise the child, and they called him by his father's name Zachary. And his mother answering, said: Not so, but he shall be called John." (Luke i. 59, 60.)

REFLECTION.—The dignity of the Christian name.

145. Why was the eighth day chosen for the circumcision of John?

Because the law of the Jews required this rite on that day, and by this the child was admitted to the covenant of God and the communion of the faithful.

146. Why was that day also taken for the naming of the child?

Among reasons given is one that it was on the day of his circumcision that God changed Abram's name to Abraham; hence all Hebrews were named when they came for this same rite.

LESSON XLIX.

TEXT.—"And they made signs to his father, how he would have him called. And demanding a writing-table, he wrote, saying: John is his name. And they all wondered. And immediately his mouth was opened, and his tongue loosed, and he spoke blessing God." (Luke i. 62–64.)

REFLECTION.—The providence of God.

147. Why did the parents insist on calling him John, notwithstanding the customs of the people?

Because it was the name given by the angel. It signifies "favor of God," or "Jehovah has had mercy."

148. How was this action received by the friends and relatives?

They had been amazed at Zachary's silence, and they were more astonished now when they heard him speak again.

149. What conclusions did they draw from all they saw and heard?

That this child, given in such a wonderful way to his

aged parents, and receiving his name from God, must be destined for a great work among men.

LESSON L.

TEXT.—"And Zachary his father was filled with the Holy Ghost: and he prophesied saying: Blessed be the Lord God of Israel, because He hath visited and wrought the redemption of His people." (Luke i. 67, 68.)

REFLECTION.—The spirit of gratitude.

150. What is the hymn of Zachary called, and why?

It is called the "Benedictus," because in Latin it begins with that word. It is recited every day in the Divine Office at Lauds.

151. When is it supposed to have been composed?

Many writers claim that Zachary composed it during the nine months of his dumbness. During this time he made deep study of the Scriptures, and learned the pure truth concerning the Messias.

152. What is the character of this hymn, and whence did it derive its inspiration?

It is called a prophecy as well as an act of thanksgiving, and derived its inspiration from the Holy Ghost, who filled Zachary with the spirit of truth, and made him not only express his gratitude, but also foretell God's future mercies.

LESSON LI.

TEXT.—"And hath raised up an horn of salvation to us: in the house of David His servant. As He spoke by the mouth of His holy prophets, who are from the beginning." (Luke i. 69, 70.)

REFLECTION.—The promise of redemption.

153. What is the first thought in the hymn of Zachary?

The opening thought is one of thankfulness (verses 68-75) for the favors bestowed on his people by the redemption. It is the grateful cry of a true Israelitish soul which has been nourished by the hopes of the Redeemer to come. He reminds them of the prophecies and types and their fulfilment.

154. What is the second thought in the hymn?

In the second part, in verses 76, 77, he turns his thought to his own son, John the Baptist, and he foretells his mission and his greatness as the prophet of the Highest and the teacher of salvation through the Messias.

155. How does he close the hymn?

He returns to the thought of gratitude in verse 78, and foretells the happiness which is dawning for those now in darkness and in evil ways. He foreshadows the dawn of a new era which is to shed its light into hearts filled with despair, and give them new hope, and warm into new life their chilled hearts.

LESSON LII.

TEXT.—"And thou child, shalt be called the prophet of the Highest: for thou shalt go before the face of the Lord to prepare His ways: To give knowledge of salvation to His people: unto the remission of their sins." (Luke i. 76, 77.)

REFLECTION.—Our duty in preparing for the Lord.

156. What is meant by prophet of the Highest?

It means that John is destined to be the prophet announcing Christ, His forerunner and the herald of His coming, preparing the way of the Lord.

157. How was he to prepare the way of the Lord?

As it was customary when the king visited the cities to have all rocks and obstacles carefully removed, and decorations tastefully placed, so John was sent to preach penance and prepare the Jewish heart to receive Christ, and finally to announce that He had come and was among them.

158. What was to be the praise accorded to him because of his work?

He was to be called by Christ "more than a prophet, a very angel sent before His face, and among the children of men there was no one greater than **John the Baptist.**" (See Matt. xi. 10, 11.)

BIBLE TALKS.

How to Interpret the Bible.

Thus far we have been led to understand the sacred character of the Bible, that it is the inspired word of God. We spoke of the inspiration of the Bible in order that we might see in what it differs from all other books ever seen or known. Now we will examine how we are to interpret it, for if it be the word of God, we must understand it as God wishes it to be understood, in order that we may find God's meaning. It would be useless to have given us the Bible, unless God also gave us a certain and unerring means of knowing its sense. Now the Bible contains truths to be believed and commands to be followed. If salvation depend upon knowing what these are, it certainly would be unjust in God to place duties upon us in such a way that we might be uncertain about them and thus endanger our salvation. Does it not seem foolish to suppose that God should give us a book and then tell us to pick from it what we are to believe and what we are to do? This would lead us to as many interpretations as there are readers, and few would agree, and what then would become of truth? No, God gave us the Bible, and it is His word; but He also gave us an unerring teacher, whose duty it is to tell what the Bible means. Some people, who believe in the Bible and nothing else, will tell you it is easy to understand it. Yet take some of the very common passages even in the discourses of Our Lord, and how many sects differ as to their meaning! St. Peter reminds his churches that in the epistles of St. Paul are "certain things **hard to be understood** which the learned and the unstable wrest, as they do also the other scriptures, to their own destruction." Evidently St. Peter did not believe in every one reading the Scriptures to suit himself. The learned Ethiopian, spoken of in the Acts of the Apostles, was trying to read the prophecy of Isaias. And Philip questioned him as to its meaning, and the answer came: "How can I understand it, unless some one show me?" Then Philip explained that it referred to Christ. Interpretation cannot depend upon the good heart or the spirit of the reader, for good men who think they are moved by the spirit of God find entirely different meanings in the very same passage. We Catholics believe that Jesus Christ established His Church upon the apostles, to whom He gave the entire deposit of faith; and this Church, speaking to us, not only tells us what the Bible is, but also what the Bible means.

PART II.

The Infancy of Christ.

The Nativity of Christ.

Read carefully and study verses 1-20 of the Second Chapter of St. Luke's gospel.

LESSON LIII.

TEXT.—"And it came to pass that in those days, there went out a decree from Cæsar Augustus, that the whole world should be enrolled." (Luke ii. 1.)

REFLECTION.—Christ's mission to men.

159. Why was this decree issued?

The Roman emperor wished this registry, it is supposed, for purposes of taxation.

160. What is meant by the whole world?

The Roman Empire, which then was the whole known world.

161. Why did each one go into his own city?

Because in the city of his ancestors the Jewish family records were kept. Romans registered in cities where they lived.

LESSON LIV.

TEXT.—" And Joseph also went up from Galilee out of the city of Nazareth into Judea, to the city of David, which is called Bethlehem: because he was of the house and family of David, to be enrolled with Mary his espoused wife." (Luke ii. 4, 5.)

REFLECTION.—Obedience to lawful authority.

162. Why did Mary and Joseph go to Bethlehem?

Because Mary was of the lineage of David, and Christ, who was to be born of her, was the heir of David's kingdom, whose city was Bethlehem.

163. What had the prophecies announced with regard to His birth?

That it would occur in Bethlehem of Juda: and hence the Jews looked to Bethlehem as the place where the Messias would be found.

164. Where was Bethlehem, and what does the word Bethlehem mean?

It was a village five or six miles south of Jerusalem. It was the town of Ruth and Booz, and the birthplace of David, whose family records it contained. Bethlehem means "house of bread," and the village was so called because of its fertility.

LESSON LV.

TEXT.—"And she brought forth her first-born Son, and wrapped Him up in swaddling-clothes, and laid Him in a manger: because there was no room for them in the inn." (Luke ii. 7.)

REFLECTION.—Humility.

165. What is meant by first-born?

It commonly refers to first-born of the father, and, as he had certain rights, it is not strange that an only son should be called the first-born.

166. What was meant by swaddling-clothes?

These were not clothes regularly made, but strips of cloth three or four inches wide and several feet long, wound around the child.

167. What do you understand by the manger?

It is supposed to have been a crib made of five small boards and placed for the use of the cattle in the limestone cave or grotto in which Christ was born.

LESSON LVI.

TEXT.—" And the angel said to them: Fear not; for behold I bring you good tidings of great joy, that shall be to all the people: for this day is born to you a Saviour, who is Christ the Lord, in the city of David." (Luke ii. 10, 11.)

REFLECTION.—Message of salvation.

168. When was Christ born?

There has been much dispute as to the exact date, but the Eastern and Western Churches seem to agree that it must have been one of the twelve nights between December 25th and January 6th. Rome held to the former, and the East held to the latter until the sixth century, when it accepted December 25th. Christ was born probably in the year 749 of Rome.

169. Who were the shepherds, and where were they located?

Tradition has it that they were natives of the little village Bethzur, near Bethlehem, in the same fields where David had served.

170. What do we see by this message to the shepherds?

That God sent the message of salvation first to the poor, and it was sent to the shepherds while they were employed in their daily work.

LESSON LVII.

TEXT.—" And suddenly there was with the angel a multitude of the heavenly army, praising God, and saying: Glory to God in the highest, and on earth peace to men of good will." (Luke ii. 13, 14.)

REFLECTION.—God's love in the salvation of men.

171. What is meant by the "heavenly army"?

It means the angels of heaven whose hosts peopled the sky above Bethlehem to do honor to the birth of their King.

172. What do you mean by "glory to God"?

God's glorious work of salvation, and the desire to spread His glory by making it known. This glory is deserving of the highest praise even in the very heavens.

173. What is understood by "peace to men of good will"?

It means that Christ has brought peace to earth, that is to say, peace to man's conscience by giving him chance for pardon, and peace between men by the law of love which He came to teach.

The Presentation.

Read carefully and study verses 22-38 of the Second Chapter of St. Luke's gospel.

LESSON LVIII.

TEXT.—"And after the days of her purification according to the law of Moses were accomplished, they carried Him to Jerusalem, to present Him to the Lord." (Luke ii. 22.)

REFLECTION.—Obedience to the law.

174. When did the event recorded in this lesson take place?

As it was an act of obedience to the law, it must have taken place forty days after the birth of Christ, and consequently before the adoration of the Magi.

175. What were the ceremonies prescribed by the law in question?

There were two ceremonies: one which demanded the purification of the mother with her gift-offering; and the other the redemption of the first-born, who was consecrated to God, or, as in the case of Jesus Christ, the presentation in the Temple.

176. Were Jesus and Mary bound by this law?

Certainly not; but they desired to show us the necessity of obedience to the law, and thus gave us an example both of obedience and poverty, for Mary made the " poor woman's offering " of two turtle-doves.

LESSON LIX.

TEXT.—" And behold there was a man in Jerusalem named Simeon, and this man was just and devout, . . . and the Holy Ghost was in him, . . . and he came by the Spirit into the Temple." (Luke ii. 25, 27.)

REFLECTION.—The beauty of sanctity.

177. Who was this Simeon spoken of in the Gospel?

He was a just and God-fearing old man, who, amid all the evils of Israel, remained faithful to God and lived in hopes of seeing the Messias. His good life was rewarded, and he appears as one of " the remnant " of which the prophet Isaias spoke.

178. How did he recognize the divine Child?

The Gospel says that the Spirit of God led him into the Temple that day and made known to him that this was the expected Messias, who was to bring salvation to mankind.

179. What other figure appears at the presentation?

A woman of extraordinary virtue, very far advanced in years, a prophetess named Anna, who spent her days in the Temple. She recognized Jesus, and gave praise to God for the redemption of Israel.

LESSON LX.

TEXT.—"Now Thou dost dismiss Thy servant, O Lord, according to Thy word, in peace: because my eyes have seen Thy salvation, which Thou hast prepared before the face of all peoples. A light to the revelation of the Gentiles, and the glory of Thy people Israel." (Luke ii. 29-32.)

REFLECTION.—Thanksgiving to God.

180. What is the hymn of holy Simeon called?

It is called the "Nunc Dimittis," from the Latin words with which it opens. They mean, "Now thou dost dismiss."

181. What is the principal thought in this hymn?

That Jesus is the source of all good. He gives (1) happiness,—"in peace"; (2) salvation,—"Thy salvation"; (3) light.—"a light to the nations"; (4) glory, —"the glory of Thy people."

182. What followed Simeon's hymn?

He gives an aged saint's blessing to the parents of this wonderful Child.

LESSON LXI.

TEXT.—"And Simeon blessed them, and said to Mary His mother: Behold this Child is set for the fall and for the resurrection of many in Israel, and for a sign which shall be contradicted: and thy own soul a sword shall pierce." (Luke ii. 34, 35.)

REFLECTION.—The sorrows of Mary.

183. What is meant by Simeon's first prophecy?

It means that Christ brought ruin to the unbelieving world, and resurrection to all who believe in Him. It may also mean disappointment to those who looked for a temporal prince, and hope to those who looked for a Saviour.

184. What is meant by the prophecy of the sword?
That violent pain should pierce Mary's heart as with a dagger when she should stand under the cross. It means that Mary, the Mother of Jesus, must prepare to bear the cross with Jesus for the redemption of mankind.

185. What do you understand by the prophecy of "the sign which shall be contradicted"?
This may be taken in connection with the "revelation of many hearts," spoken of in Luke ii. 35, and means that many will not accept Jesus as Saviour, because of earthly motives, which in all time will be seen as governing men's hearts.

The Adoration of the Magi.

Read carefully and study verses 1–12 of the Second Chapter of St. Matthew's gospel.

LESSON LXII.

TEXT.—" When Jesus therefore was born in Bethlehem of Juda, in the days of King Herod, behold, there came wise men from the East to Jerusalem, saying, Where is He that is born King of the Jews?" (Matt. ii. 1, 2.)

REFLECTION.—Seeking after Christ.

186. Who is the Herod spoken of in this story?
Herod the Great, the founder of the Herod family. He was an Edomite in race, but a Jew in religion, was Roman governor of Galilee, named king of Judea by Anthony, and rebuilt the Temple of Jerusalem, which was called Herod's temple.

187. Who were the Magi, and how many came to Bethlehem?

They were Gentiles, and, as the name Magi indicates, were called wise men. They are supposed to have been priests or followers of Zoroaster, learned in the knowledge of the stars, and enjoying the respect of the people. St. Leo says, judging by the gifts they brought that there were three of them, and Venerable Bede gives their names as Melcher, Caspar, and Balthasar; but this is mere conjecture.

188. From what country did they come, and why to Jerusalem?

Some say that they came from Arabia, others from Persia or Babylonia. They were seeking the new-born King of the Jews and they naturally came to Jerusalem, because it was the capital of Judea. It was also to confound the blindness of the Jews.

LESSON LXIII.

TEXT.—"For we have seen His star in the East, and are come to adore Him." (Matt. ii. 1.)

REFLECTION.—Correspondence with grace.

189. What did they understand by His star?

They must have known the prophecy that foretold the birth of the Messias. The years spent by the Jews in the East made scholars familiar with the books of Moses and the ancient prophecies.

190. What was this prophecy?

It was uttered by Balaam and is found in Numbers xxiv. 17: "A star shall rise out of Jacob, and a sceptre shall spring up from Israel." This star was understood to indicate the birth of the Messias.

191. What was the character of this star?

It could not have been an ordinary star, and the students of astronomy that tell of a wonderful conjunction of fixed stars at that period cannot explain it. This latter may have attracted the attention of these learned men and thus led them to notice the miraculous star of Bethlehem which they followed. It is not hard to believe that God, who sent angels to herald the birth of Christ, might have made a star to guide the Gentiles to His resting-place.

LESSON LXIV.

TEXT.—"And King Herod hearing this, was troubled, and all Jerusalem with him. And assembling together all the chief priests and the scribes of the people, he inquired of them where Christ should be born." (Matt. ii. 3.)

REFLECTION.—Power of jealousy.

192. Why was Herod troubled at the words of the Magi?

Because he feared that the coming of the new King

would destroy his power, for the people hated him, and would turn against him and dethrone him.

193. What did Herod do to quiet his fears?

He summoned all who should know the law and the prophecies, and he inquired as to when Christ should be born.

194. What was their answer, and how was it received?

They answered promptly that it was in Bethlehem of Juda, as it was written by the prophet Micheas v. 2. Herod, after closely questioning the Magi, bade them go to Bethlehem and return to him with all the information they could gather.

LESSON LXV.

TEXT.—" And entering into the house, they found the Child with Mary His mother, and falling down they adored Him: and opening their treasures, they offered Him gifts, gold, frankincense, and myrrh." (Matt. ii. 11.)

REFLECTION.—Christ, our King.

195. How were the Magi guided in their onward journey?

The star which they saw in the East appeared again and led them to the very house where the child Jesus was found.

196. What is meant by their gifts?

After adoring Him as their God, according to their Eastern customs they made presents to royalty. By gold they acknowledged His kingly power; by frankincense, His divinity; and by myrrh, His humanity.

197. How did they return home, and why?

They were warned in a dream not to return to Jerusalem, but passed round by the south, and either crossed the Jordan at Jericho, or else went round the Dead Sea. They did this that Herod might not be helped in his wicked plot against Christ.

BIBLE TALKS.

How to Interpret the Bible. (*Continued.*)

We have already spoken about the necessity of having some one with authority from God to tell us what the Bible means. We know that, more than all other writings, the Holy Scriptures are obscure and difficult to understand. We easily see the reason for this if we remember that in great part they are older than the oldest secular books. They contain much sublime thought and expression, and they were written by men and for peoples whose modes of speech and habits of life were entirely different from ours. The style at times is elegant and poetic, and at times simple and negligent. The languages in which they were written are very far from ours, and the versions often contain the idioms and quaint sayings of the original language. Who is there who can go back to the original to find if the translations are correct? Who can settle disputes? Who can determine what God means to have us believe? Since it is God's word, God must have fixed some certain way of letting us know what His words mean. The Jews of old had this means of knowledge in the synagogue, and Christ placed it in His Church, to which He gave all power to teach the world what to believe and what to do. Now, there is in the Church a central standard of interpretation, which is that body of doctrine of which the apostolic teaching is composed and which the different apostles delivered to the churches established by them. This body of doctrine has been preserved by tradition and kept from error by the infallibility with which our good Saviour has invested His Church when He promised to be with her all days, and that the gates of hell should not prevail against her. To this body of doctrine, which is called the deposit of faith, all interpretations must conform. Hence, no meaning should be given to any part of the Bible that would be opposed to any part of these doctrines. Even in the days of the apostles, the Council of the Church was the interpreter of the Scriptures, and to it belonged the sole right of decision. When in the early Church, there was difference as to the meaning of certain laws for the newly converted Jews, the Council of Jerusalem was called, and it decided the dispute. The Scriptures were not so clear to the Jews, for although their learned doctors told them when Christ was to be born, yet they failed to accept Him, and by the very Scriptures they asked that He be crucified. As Catholics, we believe that Christ established His Church and gave to it not only the mission to teach the world His doctrine, but also to guard His word from being misunderstood. When, then, we ask the Church what we are bound to believe about God and our duties, we believe that she cannot err in what she tells us. When we go to her and ask what the Bible means in this or that passage, we believe that she alone can tell us the true meaning, for she alone is the Church of Christ, and she can no more err than Christ Himself.

The Flight into Egypt.

Read carefully and study verses 13-23 of the Second Chapter of St. Matthew's gospel.

LESSON LXVI.

TEXT.—"And after they were departed, behold an angel of the Lord appeared in sleep to Joseph, saying: Arise, and take the Child and His mother, and fly into Egypt, and be there until I shall tell thee." (Matt. ii. 13.)

REFLECTION.—The ministry of angels.

198. When did the angel appear, directing Joseph to Egypt?

Immediately after the departure of the Magi, who did not return to Herod at Jerusalem as he had requested.

199. Why was Egypt selected as a refuge for the Holy Family?

Because it was at this time a Roman province near Palestine, and was at all times a place of refuge for persecuted Jews, and hence was largely peopled by them.

200. What was the prophecy that referred to this?
Osee xi. 2: "Out of Egypt have I called My Son." This prophecy refers to the people of Israel, freed from

captivity, but more particularly to Christ called out of Egypt by God.

LESSON LXVII.

TEXT.—"For it will come to pass that Herod will seek the Child to destroy Him. Who arose and took the Child and His mother by night and retired into Egypt." (Matt. ii. 13, 14.)

REFLECTION.—Sin, the Herod of the soul.

201. Why was Joseph ordered to fly into Egypt?
To escape the jealousy of Herod, who was angered because the Magi did not return to him as he had demanded.

202. What was the motive of Herod's jealousy and hatred?

He feared that Christ was to be the King of Judea and rule in his place.

203. How did Joseph receive the message?

Humbly trusting in divine Providence, he promptly and generously obeyed, and immediately went from Bethlehem.

LESSON LXVIII.

TEXT.—" And he [Joseph] was there until the death of Herod: that it might be fulfilled which the Lord spoke by the prophet, saying: Out of Egypt have I called My Son." (Matt. ii. 15.)

REFLECTION.—Promptness in obedience.

204. When and how did the Holy Family journey to Egypt?

Probably the very night the message came, in order to avoid the threatening danger to the Child. The road selected was the one by Joppe, which would be the way least suspected.

205. Why did Herod decree the massacre of the innocents?

In order that by this cruel act he might reach Christ and destroy Him.

206. How many children were put to death by this order?

It is thought that between twenty and thirty were massacred, as that would be about the proportion of male infants in Bethlehem's population, which at that time was about 2000.

LESSON LXIX.

TEXT.—" Then was fulfilled that which was spoken by Jeremias the prophet, saying: A voice in Rama was heard, lamentation and great mourning: Rachel bewailing her children, and would not be comforted, because they are not." (Matt. ii. 17, 18.)

REFLECTION.—The Church weeps for sinners.

207. Where is Rama, and what is here referred to?

Rama was a village in the territory of Benjamin, about five miles north of Jerusalem. It was there that many Benjamites were massacred, when, under Nabuzardan, B.C. 586, many were imprisoned at Rama before their transfer to Babylon.

208. What do you understand by the reference to Rachel?

Rachel was the mother of the tribe of Benjamin, and her tomb was close to Bethlehem. She is represented by the prophet as mourning for her captive children.

209. How is the prophecy fulfilled in the massacre of the holy innocents?

As Rachel mourned her children of Benjamin at Rama, so her grief is renewed by the slaughter at Bethlehem, and is all the greater because it is an attempt to kill the Messias, the hope of Israel and the pride of the tribe of Benjamin.

LESSON LXX.

TEXT.—" Who arose, and took the Child and His mother, and came into the land of Israel. But hearing that Archelaus reigned in Judea in the room of Herod his father, he was afraid to go thither: and being warned in sleep, retired into the quarters of Galilee." (Matt. ii. 21, 22.)

REFLECTION.—Parental responsibility.

210. How long did they remain in Egypt, and when did they return?

Herod died in Jericho, April, year of Rome 750, a few

weeks after the massacre, and it is thought that the Holy Family returned in a few months, although some fix it at two or three years.

211. How did they return, and why not to Bethlehem?

Tradition tells us that they returned by Ascalon, Joppe, and Cesarea. Fearing that Archelaus, Herod's son, was as wicked as his father, Joseph, under divine guidance, went into Galilee and took up his home in Nazareth, so that the prophecy of the "despised Nazarene" might be fulfilled.

212. Are there not legends connected with the flight into Egypt?

Most beautiful ones, that tell of the trees bearing their fruits and bending their branches to nourish Jesus, the wild beasts adoring, the roses of Jericho blossoming, and the idols falling in Egypt.

PART III.

The Youth of Christ.

The Boyhood of Christ.

Read carefully and study verse 23 of the Second Chapter of St. Matthew's gospel and verses 40–43 of the Second Chapter of St. Luke's gospel.

LESSON LXXI.

TEXT.—"And coming He dwelt in a city called Nazareth: that it might be fulfilled which was said by the prophets: That He shall be called a Nazarite." (Matt. ii. 23.)

REFLECTION.—Humility brings glory.

213. Where do you find the prophecy referred to above, and what does it mean?

It is not found in any prophet in those words. The Gospel sums up a number of predictions which refer to Nazareth, either in its signification, which means *branch*, or because the prophet called Him "despised," and Nazareth was a term of contempt.

214. Where is Nazareth, and why this contempt for it?

Nazareth is a city twenty miles east of the Mediterranean or Great Sea, sixteen miles west of the Sea of Galilee, and about seventy miles from Jerusalem. It passed into disrepute either because it was in Galilee, which was despised by Judeans, or because, being near to the heathen, its morals were lax.

215. How was the youth of Jesus passed in Nazareth?

Under the direction of His parents, in the home and the workshop or among His companions. He was taught the Old Testament, and practised the trade of carpenter, helping Joseph, who provided for the Holy Family.

LESSON LXXII.

TEXT.—" And the Child grew, and waxed strong, full of wisdom: and the grace of God was in Him. And His parents went every year to Jerusalem, at the solemn day of the pasch." (Luke ii. 40, 41.)

REFLECTION.—Christian childhood.

216. How often in the year did the Law of Moses oblige attendance at the Temple?

All adult males were bound to appear before the Lord, at the altar, three times in the year—at the festival of Passover, Pentecost, and Tabernacles. Devout women went when they could.

THE BOYHOOD OF CHRIST. 77

217. Why did they go to Jerusalem?

Because there was but one Temple, and that was in Jerusalem. Between two and three million Jews attended these feasts every year.

218. What did the Passover commemorate?

It commemorated the salvation of Israel from the exterminating angel, who, while slaying the first-born of the Egyptians, passed over the marked houses of the Jews. It began at sunset on the 14th day of Nisan (our Easter) and lasted seven days, during which only unleavened bread was prescribed. (See Deut. xvi. 2; Exod. xii. 15 and xxxiv. 18.)

LESSON LXXIII.

TEXT.—"And when He was twelve years old, they going up into Jerusalem according to the custom of the feast." (Luke ii. 42.)

REFLECTION.—Parental example.

219. Why did Jesus go to the Temple at His twelfth year?

Because at twelve a Jewish boy was supposed to know the law. He then became known as a "son of the law," and he was bound to follow it.

220. What did Jewish parents consider as a duty to their children?

To teach them the history and laws of Israel, to have them commit to memory the precepts, and attend the daily and special services in the synagogues and the feasts in the Temple.

221. What was the one book they taught and studied?

The Old Testament, or, as they called it, the "Book of Laws," which contained the history of their people and the laws of God.

LESSON LXXIV.

TEXT.—"And having fulfilled the days, when they returned, the child Jesus remained in Jerusalem, and His parents knew it not." (Luke ii. 43.)

REFLECTION.—Parental care.

222. What is meant by the fulfilment of the days?
The time prescribed by law. The feast lasted seven days, but those who wished to return home sooner were allowed to do so after three days.

223. How can you account for the fact that the parents of Jesus did not miss Him?
They had perfect confidence in Him, and supposed Him with other boys or with acquaintances. The crowds were so great and there was so much confusion in Jerusalem that it was very difficult to keep families together.

224. Who were the rulers of Judea at that time?
Augustus Cæsar was emperor of Rome, Coponius governor of Judea, and Herod Antipater, son of Herod the Great, ruler of Galilee and Perea.

BIBLE TALKS.

Bible Geography.

The country made famous by the birth of Christ is Palestine, about which it is well for you to learn something. Palestine in the Gospel times was an irregular strip of land bordering the southeastern shore of the Mediterranean Sea. In the days of Solomon, one thousand years before Christ, it contained sixty thousand square miles, but at the time of Christ, under Herod the Great, it had but twelve thousand miles of territory. On the north of Palestine were Syria and Phœnicia; the Arabian desert was on the east, the wilderness of Sinai on the south, and the Mediterranean Sea on the west. It was one hundred and fifty miles in length and ninety miles wide at the southern end, which was the widest part. The river Jordan, rising in the northern mountains, flowed southerly nearly the entire length of the land, one hundred and thirty-four miles, and emptied into the Dead Sea, passing through two lakes, Lake Merom and the Sea of Galilee, both in the north. Palestine had several mountains. Near the Sea of Galilee was Mount Thabor. In the centre was Mount Garizim, two thousand eight hundred and fifty feet high, and near Jerusalem was the Mount of Olives, while Jerusalem itself was built chiefly on Mount Zion.

In the time of Christ Palestine was divided into four principal provinces, three west of the Jordan and one east of it. The western countries were Judea in the south, Galilee in the north, and Samaria in the centre, with Perea on the east. Perea is often said to include the countries north of it, such as Auranitis and Trachonitis. Fix these geographical ideas in your mind, so that you may follow the Gospel story intelligently.

Jesus in the Temple.

Read carefully and study verses 44–52 of the Second Chapter of the gospel according to St. Luke.

LESSON LXXV.

Text.—"And it came to pass, that after three days they found Him in the Temple sitting in the midst of the doctors, hearing them and asking them questions." (Luke ii. 46.)

Reflection.—The Catechism teaching.

225. Who were the doctors who were in the Temple at that time?

They were the authorized interpreters and teachers of the law which the Jews were obliged to follow. They were also known as Scribes, and the most absolute reverence was given to them by all their pupils.

226. Where in the Temple is this scene thought to have taken place?

In one of the courts or chambers of the Temple, where on feast-days the doctors of the law allowed free discussion and an opportunity was given for inquiry. When teaching with authority the Scribes were said to occupy the chair of Moses, and the scholars sat about them.

227. Were these eminent rabbis or teachers present on this occasion?

It is supposed that some of the learned teachers of that year were there, and among them were Hillel, Shammai, and Nicodemus, who were famous doctors of the law. They were amazed at the knowledge of Jesus.

LESSON LXXVI.

Text.—"And seeing Him, they [Joseph and Mary] wondered. And His mother said to Him: Son, why hast Thou done so to us? behold Thy father and I have sought Thee sorrowing." (Luke ii. 48.)

Reflection.—Maternal solicitude.

228. Why did the holy parents wonder at the knowledge of Jesus?

Because it was the first revelation of His divine power. He who was so mild and submissive, a mere child, confused the venerable doctors of the Temple whom the Galileans revered as prodigies of learning and authority.

229. Why does the complaint come from the Blessed Mother?

Because St. Joseph, being only a protector and foster-father, yields to Mary, whose maternal heart leads her to seem to chide her divine Son for His apparent negligence.

230. Did she not know His divine character, and why therefore did she sorrow for Him?

Because He was placed in her care to be educated, and she had to use all natural means to that end, and her motherly instincts manifested themselves.

LESSON LXXVII.

TEXT.—"And He said to them: How is it that you sought Me? did you not know, that I must be about My Father's business? And they understood not the word that He spoke unto them." (Luke ii. 49, 50.)

REFLECTION.—Our duty to God, our Father.

231. What makes this answer remarkable?

1. It is the first word of Our Saviour which is recorded.

2. It expresses the idea that God is our true Father, and to serve Him in His temple is deserving of praise and not of blame.

3. It is an abridgment of the Gospel, in the Incarnation and redemption.

232. How do you find the truth of the Incarnation and redemption in those words?

The words "My Father" express very strongly that Christ is the Son of God and hence He possesses a divine and human nature. *My*, and not *our*, makes it personal. "My Father's *business*" indicates the truth and justice of God as manifested in sending His Son to redeem man.

233. Can you regard this answer as a reprimand to the Blessed Mother?

Some non-Catholics who do not understand the true relations of the Blessed Mother to her Son Jesus regard it as such. Christ reminds His parents that they should look for Him in the Temple; but His docility in leaving the Temple, going to Nazareth, and spending with them the eighteen years that followed before His public life shows His love and obedience, which cannot be reconciled with a reprimand.

LESSON LXXVIII.

TEXT.—"And they understood not the word that He spoke unto them. And He went down with them, and came to Nazareth: and was subject to them. And His mother kept all these words in her heart. And Jesus advanced in wisdom and age, and grace with God and men." (Luke ii. 50–52.)

REFLECTION.—Obedience to parents.

234. How was it that they did not understand His words?

Though His parents knew His real character, yet they seemed to be ignorant of the means to be used for man's redemption, and did not realize that this visit to the Temple had a bearing on the work.

235. Why did the Blessed Mother ponder over these words?

Because she recalled the words of Simeon and also the words of the angel, and a greater insight seemed to come to her as to the mystery of redemption and her part in the scheme of salvation.

236. What do we know of the subsequent years of Christ's private life?

It is all summed up in the Gospel narrative. "He went down to Nazareth and was subject to them." Jesus obeyed

Mary and Joseph, worked with them and for them. "He advanced in wisdom," which means that His natural wisdom increased with experience and all revered Him, while in humility He prepared Himself for public life by eighteen years of privacy.

BIBLE TALKS.

Jewish Customs for Youth.

At twelve or thirteen years of age every Jewish boy was considered a man, for he was then admitted as a member of the community of Israel, and he bound himself to follow the law. He then began to wear what were called "frontlets" or "phylacteries," observed the fasts, and went to Jerusalem for the feasts. These frontlets were little strips of parchment attached by straps to the arms and head. On them were written four passages from the Old Testament (Exodus xiii. 2-10, 11-17; Deuteronomy vi. 4-9, 13-23) which reminded them of their duty to God in sacrifice and love. A special ink was used in the transcribing of these verses from the Scriptures. Rolled in a case of black calfskin, one set was attached to the left arm, while another was put into four little cells within a square case, and attached to the forehead by two leathern thongs, on which Hebrew letters were written. The journeys to Jerusalem were in the nature of pilgrimages, and were a prominent feature of the religious life of the Jews. Caravans went from the different sections where the Jews dwelt, and it is stated that at the Passover, which is the feast mentioned in our lesson, no less than two million Jews were in Jerusalem. Jesus and the caravan of Nazareth came by Sichem and the well of Jacob. The Temple, which held over two hundred thousand people, was crowded, the priests offered the victims of sacrifice, and the people prayed. The doctors of the law taught the people their duties, and reminded them of their traditions, while moments were given for discussion.

Preaching of John in the Desert.

Read and study verses 1-17 of the Third Chapter of St. Matthew's gospel; also verses 2-11 of the First Chapter of St. Mark's gospel, and verses 7-22 of the Third Chapter of St. Luke's gospel.

LESSON LXXIX.

TEXT.—" And in those days cometh John the Baptist preaching in the desert of Judea, and saying : Do penance : for the kingdom of heaven is at hand." (Matt. iii. 1, 2.)

REFLECTION.—The necessity of penance.

237. Who was John the Baptist ?

As we have seen in a preceding lesson he was a prophet, the son of Zachary and Elizabeth, a cousin of Our Lord, and the one chosen to announce the coming of the Redeemer.

238. Why was he called the Baptist?

Because he obliged his disciples to be baptized as a mark of their repentance.

239. How did this baptism compare with Christian Baptism?

As the shadow with the substance, as the figure with the reality. It only purified or signified purification as a mere ceremony, but did not regenerate. It was a preparation for what was to come with Christ.

LESSON LXXX.

TEXT.—"Then went out to him Jerusalem and all Judea, and all the country about Jordan; and were baptized by him in the Jordan confessing their sins." (Matt. iii. 5, 6.)

REFLECTION.—The confession of sin.

240. How was John the Baptist clothed, and what was his food?

He was clothed in a plain garment made from camel's hair, and his food was locusts and wild honey, such as were used by the poorer classes because of their cheapness.

241. Why did he live in this way?

Probably in imitation of the prophets of old, as also to rebuke the arrogant and rich about him, and to foreshadow the poverty of the Redeemer.

242. What drew the great crowds to John?

He appeared as a prophet and as a Nazarite; his hair was uncut, his beard unshaven, and his preaching was full of earnestness and conviction, which touched the hearts of the multitudes, who just at that time were expecting the Messias.

LESSON LXXXI.

TEXT.—"For this is He that was spoken of by Isaias the prophet, saying: A voice of one crying in the desert: Prepare ye the way of the Lord: make straight His paths." (Matt. iii. 3.)

REFLECTION.—The wilderness of sin.

243. Which was the wilderness referred to?

The wilderness of Judea, which was a wild, hilly region extending from Hebron to the Dead Sea. It was not a desert.

244. What did they understand by the words, "make straight His paths"?

That as mighty kings, by their armies, had the roads made or straightened and the valleys filled before their triumphal march, so the lives of sinners should be changed in order that the great King might be able to reach their hearts.

245. How did John the Baptist prepare the way of the Lord?

By warning the people of the near approach of Christ, crying out against sin and urging all to repentance, that their hearts might thus be prepared for the graces of redemption.

LESSON LXXXII.

TEXT.—"And seeing many of the Pharisees and Sadducees coming to his baptism, he said to them: Ye brood of vipers, who hath showed you to flee from the wrath to come?" (Matt. iii. 7.)

REFLECTION.—The punishment of hypocrisy.

246. Who were the Pharisees?

The sect among the Jews aiming to observe the letter of the Mosaic law and the unwritten traditions. They condemned all who did not agree with them, and believed in immortality and the existence of the angels.

247. Who were the Sadducees?

A sect among the Jews, and composed largely of priests. They accepted the Books of Moses, rejected oral tradition, and denied immortality, as also the existence of angels. They bitterly opposed the Pharisees.

248. Why did John the Baptist denounce them even as they came to him?

Because, knowing their deceit, he realized that they came to be baptized but not to repent. They were ready to accept new ceremonies, but not to lead a new life. He condemned their hypocrisy and dishonesty.

LESSON LXXXIII.

TEXT.—" I indeed baptize you in water unto penance: but He that shall come after me is mightier than I, whose shoes I am not worthy to bear: He shall baptize you in the Holy Ghost and fire." (Matt. iii. 11.)

REFLECTION.—John's humility.

249. To whom does John refer in these words, "He that shall come"?

He refers to Christ, who, as indicated by the word "come," was already there, and, directing attention from himself and his works, which excited wonder and admiration, he fixes their thought on the greatness of the Messias.

250. How does John show his insignificance in comparison with Christ?

By asserting his unworthiness even to carry or loose the sandals of Christ, which was a task assigned to the lowest menial of the household.

251. How does John magnify the baptism which Christ is to administer?

He shows that it is not a mere ceremony or symbol, as his was, but the reality by which the Holy Spirit will enter into man's soul, to be as a fire, purifying, enlightening, and regenerating man.

BIBLE TALKS.

Nazareth and the Education of the Jews.

To the Christian child there is no city that has such beautiful memories as Nazareth, for it was the home of our dear Saviour, who passed His childhood and youth within its precincts. Everything about this ancient city reminds the traveller of something in the life of Christ. Nazareth was a great centre of Jewish Temple life, for one of the "courses" of the priesthood centred there, and went from there in a body to Jerusalem. Its inhabitants were principally Jews, although some Gentiles had found a home among them. The traditions of the people were closely allied with the strict observances of Judaism. Until the child reached his fifth year, he was by right under the direction of the mother. Then the father began his instruction in the law of God and the profession which he himself followed. Education was imposed on the people as a sacred duty. Conscience was the main object of the parental instruction. To engrave on it the law of God, and with love for God a love for Israel, was the main duty of the Jewish home. The Jewish law never ceased to urge the father to teach his son on all occasions, at home or in travelling, what God required and what God had done. Another great lesson was taught by the law, and that was to honor and obey one's parents. There were three places where the Jewish child received instruction—the home, the synagogue, and the workshop. At home his parents taught him his duties, at the synagogue he learned the law, and at the shop a trade was taught him. Joseph's carpenter shop was Christ's first school, for in His day there were no schools in Nazareth. At His work He heard the Scriptures read and He learned the history of His people, for thus He wished by ordinary and natural means to grow into the knowledge which became Him as the Saviour of Israel. How we may imagine the Holy Family praying for the redemption of Israel, reciting the psalms, and finding in one another the earthly happiness promised to fidelity! Nazareth had a synagogue, **to which Jesus went with His parents on the Sabbath and other** appointed days. There they prayed at morning, noon, and evening. There Jesus heard the readers interpret the verses which they read from the Torah, or Book of the Law, and He heard His own destiny carefully outlined. Thus He increased in knowledge, while the practical side of life was attended to in the hours at the carpenter's trade in the humble workshop of His father. Thus Nazareth comes to the Christian child as the home of the child Jesus, and is dearer to his faith than any other spot on earth.

PART IV.

Preparation for Public Life.

The Baptism of Jesus in the Jordan.

Read carefully and study verses 13–17 of the Third Chapter of St. Matthew's gospel, verses 9–11 of the First Chapter of St. Mark's gospel, and verses 21, 22 of the Third Chapter of St. Luke's gospel.

LESSON LXXXIV.

TEXT.—"Then cometh Jesus from Galilee to the Jordan, unto John, to be baptized by him." (Matt. iii. 13.)

REFLECTION.—Humility of Christ.

252. How old was Christ when He came to be baptized by John?

He was probably about thirty years of age, which was the age prescribed for the Levites to enter upon their ministry, and of the rabbis to become teachers.

253. Where did Christ come from, and where did the baptism take place?

He came from Nazareth, where He had lived with His parents in quiet and obscurity. It is thought that the baptism took place at one of the fords of the Jordan, near Jericho, at a place called by some Bethabara and by others Bethany.

254. Why did Jesus seek to be baptized?

Although He had no sin, yet He thus publicly renounced all sin, sanctioned penance, and gave an example to all those who were to follow Him, that these were means of preparation for the mission of teachers.

LESSON LXXXV.

TEXT.—"But John stayed Him, saying: I ought to be baptized by Thee, and comest Thou to me?" (Matt. iii. 14.)

REFLECTION.—Man as an instrument of grace.

255. What impelled John to forbid Jesus to seek baptism from him?

The greatness of Him whom he knew to be his Lord and Master caused him, in his humility, to disclaim any right to perform a religious ceremony of sin-purification for One who was absolutely sinless.

256. What answer came to John from Christ?

The reminder that this act was in conformity with the will of God, and that example might be given to others of the necessity of obedience to the law and the ceremonies.

257. What followed after this?

John baptized Jesus, and then came the first public manifestation of the true character of the Messias.

LESSON LXXXVI.

TEXT.—"And Jesus being baptized, forthwith came out of the water; and lo the heavens were opened to Him: and He saw the Spirit of God descending as a dove, and coming upon Him." (Matt. iii. 16.)

REFLECTION.—Effect of the Holy Spirit on us.

258. Who were witnesses to this manifestation of divine approval?

Jesus Himself, as He came from the water, and John, who was privileged to witness the same sight, as St. John testifies in his gospel (i. 32).

259. What is meant by the dove descending upon Jesus?

It symbolizes God the Holy Ghost, who in the bodily shape of a dove, which always represents peace and love, came from heaven to make known the Godhead in Christ.

260. Whom did the voice saying, "This is My beloved Son" represent?

It represented God the Father, the First Person of the Blessed Trinity, who thus publicly made known the presence of the Second Person of the Trinity, who was Jesus Christ His Son, upon whom the Holy Ghost, the Third Person, had just descended. It proclaimed Jesus as the Messias, the One in whom the Father was well pleased.

LESSON LXXXVII.

TEXT.—"And behold a voice from heaven saying: This is My beloved Son, in whom I am well pleased." (Matt. iii. 17.)

REFLECTION.—The Christian, child of God.

261. At what other times in Christ's life was the silence broken by the voice from heaven?

Once at the Transfiguration (Mark ix. 17), and once in the courts of the Temple during the Passion (John xii. 28).

262. Why did God do these extraordinary things?

To publicly announce the mission of Jesus, to give God's sanction to Him, and to make John and the people satisfied that Jesus was indeed the Messias.

263. When was the mission of John the Baptist to end?

When he would present Christ to the Jews, call Him the Lamb of God, and tell that he had seen the Spirit of God descend upon Him.

The Temptation of Jesus.

Read carefully and study verses 1–11 of the Fourth Chapter of St. Matthew's gospel, verses 12, 13 of the First Chapter of St. Mark, and verses 1–13 of the Fourth Chapter of St. Luke.

LESSON LXXXVIII.

TEXT.—"Then Jesus was led by the Spirit into the desert, to be tempted by the devil. And when He had fasted forty days and forty nights, afterwards He was hungry." (Matt. iv. 1, 2.)

REFLECTION.—Fasting, a means of sanctification.

264. What is the meaning of the words "led by the Spirit to be tempted"?

It means that after the baptism and the divine manifestation a divine impulse urged Jesus to put His life to the test and face the worst trials to which as man He could be exposed.

265. Who is the devil here referred to?
He is the spirit of evil, the enemy of God and man, sometimes called the demon, whose nature is spiritual and intelligent. Here he appears for the first time in the Gospel to thwart the designs of redemption. He was once a good angel, but he lost his innocence and heaven by his rebellion against God.

266. Why did Jesus allow Himself to be tempted?
To show us that temptation is not sin, and that all men can resist temptation if they pray to God and mortify themselves. The grace of God comes by prayer and fasting, both of which are necessary for the victory.

LESSON LXXXIX.

Text.—"And the tempter coming said to Him: If Thou be the Son of God, command that these stones be made bread. Who answered and said: It is written: Not in bread alone doth man live, but in every word that proceedeth from the mouth of God." (Matt. iv. 3, 4.)

Reflection.—God's word is true food.

267. To what weakness of humanity does Satan address himself in this first temptation?
To the sensual appetites, for the devil waited until Jesus was exhausted from hunger. He appealed to Him to relieve His hunger and at the same time to show His divine power.

268. Why does the devil quote the Scripture?
In order to make it appear that the act would be entirely proper, as it had God's approval in the Scripture.

269. How does Jesus answer the temptation and foil the devil?
He refuses to assert His divine power, and simply quotes the Scripture, which tells that man needs something more for his life than the bread for which his body craves. The word of God is the truest food.

LESSON XC.

Text.—"Then the devil took Him up into the holy city, and set Him upon the pinnacle of the Temple, and said to Him: If Thou be the Son of God, cast Thyself down. For it is written: That He hath given His angels charge over Thee, and in their hands shall they bear Thee up, lest perhaps Thou dash Thy foot against a stone." (Matt. iv. 5, 6.)

Reflection.—We must not tempt God.

270. What is here meant by the "pinnacle of the Temple"?
Probably a high point of the building, either Solomon's

porch on the east side, or at the middle elevation on the royal porch. The former looked down into the valley of the Cedron, three hundred and thirty feet below, and the latter into the valley of Hinnom, six hundred feet below. The roof was flat, surrounded by a balustrade.

271. To what does Satan appeal in this temptation?
He appeals to pride, that He may thus easily succeed in His mission; for if Christ relies on His heavenly Father He will prove to all the people that He is sent from God and is the expected Redeemer.

272. How did Jesus answer this temptation?
Reminding the devil that it is forbidden to tempt God, He condemns the plan of gaining even what may be good and desirable by means that are false and forbidden.

LESSON XCI.

Text.—"Again the devil took Him up into a very high mountain: and showed Him all the kingdoms of the world, and the glory of them, and said to Him: All these will I give Thee, if falling down, Thou wilt adore me." (Matt. iv. 8, 9.)

Reflection.—Worldly ambition.

273. What mountain is here referred to?
There is much dispute as to the particular mountain. Many claim it to be one called Quarantania, from the top of which many countries may be seen. Others consider that by some angelic manifestation He was led to think of all the kingdoms placed in review before Him.

274. How did Satan pretend to make gift of all kingdoms to Him?
By very stupidly representing himself as a messenger from God, and offering Him a temporal kingdom in exchange for the spiritual one of His heart.

275. To what did Satan appeal by this third temptation?

To the ambition of one who wanted to rule the nations, which he knew was the desire of the Jewish people in their Messias. Satan promised all the temporal power possible on condition that Jesus would give him the love of His heart; but Jesus spurned the offer, and taught Satan the great law of the adoration of God alone.

LESSON XCII.

TEXT.—"Then the devil left Him: and behold angels came and ministered to Him." (Matt. iv. 11.)

REFLECTION.—God rewards the faithful servant.

276. When did these temptations occur, and how are they to be classed?

Some assert that they occurred at intervals during the time Jesus spent in the desert; others that they came in rapid succession, just as the Evangelists relate; others that they were only internal. They are classed as uniting in one great effort to conquer Christ, and hence they are called "the temptation."

277. Did Satan appear visibly to Christ, and are we to take the text literally?

There are many who answer affirmatively to both questions; others, with Origen and St. Cyprian, maintain that the temptations were prompted by Satan to the mind and heart of Jesus, while the tempter did not appear, and that the Gospel uses a vivid picture to impress men with the designs of the evil spirit.

278. How can you explain Satan's action towards Christ, since Christ is incapable of evil?

It can be explained only by the feeling of doubt which possessed the devil as to Christ's real character. Christ's answers gave him no knowledge of His divinity.

BIBLE TALKS.

Journeys of Jesus.

Our divine Saviour had passed His boyhood and youth at Nazareth with His parents, following the humble avocation of a carpenter. When the time came for His public life, in His twenty-ninth year, He left home to go to John the Baptist for baptism. Leaving Nazareth, He went east about twenty miles, crossed the river Jordan, entering Decapolis, and went south through the Jordan valley by the east side of the river about sixty-five miles, until He reached a place called Bethabara, and there, at one of the fords of the Jordan, He was baptized. Bethabara was about five miles northeast of Jericho, and is now known as Nimrin. The oldest manuscripts and the Vulgate call it Bethany, and this agrees with the traditions of the Latin Church, although Origen says it was Bethabara, because he could find no trace of Bethany, which might have disappeared before his time, owing to the many wars to which that country was subjected. Bethabara, in Hebrew, means the House of the Passage, and Bethany, the House of Dates. After His baptism Jesus crossed the Jordan and entered the Judean wilderness, where He began His fast of forty days and where He met the great temptation. This desert was in all probability the uninhabited and hilly country lying between Jerusalem and Jericho, and commonly called Quarantania. It was a part of the wilderness of Judea between those two cities on the west and the upper part of the Dead Sea and the Jordan on the east side. The name Quarantania, which means a space of forty days, is thought to have come from Christ's fast of forty days in one of its caves. It was here that Christ buried Himself from the world, to give Himself up to prayer and fasting, in order to prepare Himself for His great mission. This desert has had many hermits since, who have peopled its many caves and lived in imitation of Christ.

Review.

LESSON XCIII.

TEXT.—"For there is no other name under heaven given to men, whereby we must be saved." (Acts iv. 12.)

REFLECTION.—The sweet name of Jesus.

279. Give a general appreciation of the work done in study of the birth, youth, and early life of Our Saviour.

280. When, and where, was Christ born, and what were the circumstances of His birth? (Page 58.)

281. What do you understand by the presentation of Our Lord, and what were the incidents connected with it? (Page 62.)

LESSON XCIV.

TEXT.—"The kings of Tharsis and the islands shall offer presents; the kings of the Arabians and of Saba shall bring gifts." (Psa. lxxi. 10.)

REFLECTION.—Mankind worshipping the Redeemer.

282. Describe the visit of the Magi. (Page 65.)

283. What was the flight into Egypt, and why was it undertaken? (Page 70.)

284. Mention some incidents in the boyhood of Christ. (Page 75.)

LESSON XCV.

TEXT.—"And He went down with them, and came to Nazareth; and was subject to them." (Luke ii. 51.)

REFLECTION.—Filial reverence.

285. Tell the incident called "Jesus in the Temple." (Page 79.)

286. Where did John the Baptist exercise his ministry, and what were the characteristics of it? (Page 84.)

287. Describe the baptism of Christ in the Jordan. (Page 90.)

LESSON XCVI.

TEXT.—"Be gone Satan: for it is written: The Lord thy God shalt thou adore, and Him only shalt thou serve." (Matt. iv. 10.)

REFLECTION.—Adoration belongs to God alone.

288. Analyze the great temptation and explain it. (Page 93.)

289. Tell something of education among the Jews. (Page 88.)

290. Describe some one of the journeys of Jesus as studied in the preceding pages. (Page 98.)

BIBLE TALKS.

The Bible and Tradition.

We have seen how necessary it is to have the finger of God pointing out to us the meaning of His holy word. The standard of interpretation by which we can see God's meaning is found in the sacred deposit of faith received by the apostles from Jesus Christ. Now we are not depending upon this one book, even though that book be the Bible. All sacred truth is not in it, although all that is in it is sacred truth. The Church teaches us that there is besides the Bible that which is known as tradition. We will explain what is meant by tradition, and we will see how the Bible needs tradition in order that we may know the whole truth. What is tradition? It is the body of truths belonging to faith and morals, some of which are not clearly stated in Scripture, but given by word of mouth from Christ to the apostles and by them handed down in continued succession. We remember that St. John, at the close of his gospel, says there is much not written and which if written would fill many books. The apostles received from Christ much which they did not commit to writing, and yet this was divine truth equally with the written word. Their disciples received these unwritten messages and treasured them as apostolical traditions. It is that to which St. Paul refers when he urges the Thessalonians "to stand fast and hold the traditions which they had learned, whether by word or by our epistles." It was divine tradition, received from the elders, which led the Jews to receive as the word of God the canon of Scripture and the Mosaic law. Tradition tells us of the abolition of the Sabbath and the institution of the Sunday, and it is authority for infant baptism and for the settlement of the famous controversy of rebaptizing as urged between St. Augustine and St. Cyprian. It was not in the economy of redemption that any one book should contain all the doctrine of salvation, or that any book was to be man's sole guide in faith and morals.

From the beginning the truths of religion had been preserved by tradition, which, carried from patriarchal line to prophetical, were not gathered in a book until Moses wrote twenty-five hundred years after Adam. But there was an unbroken tradition from father to son, from family to family, by which men knew the will of God and the truths of religion. When Christ came, He selected disciples, and from them apostles; He conversed with them and instructed them in the mysteries of God. To them He gave His power and His mission, and He sent them to preach everywhere, teaching mankind what He had commanded them and promising to be with them always, and that He would send the Spirit of truth to teach them truth and abide with them forever. Their mission was to teach and man's duty was to obey them if he would be saved. "He that heareth you heareth Me." Christ wrote nothing, neither did He commission them to write. Christ preached, the apostles preached. Occasion demanded letters to the churches established, or circumstances led to the recording of events in the life of Christ and the apostles. Nowhere can we find any evidence that all was written, or that any book was intended to be the sole rule of life. St. John Chrysostom says: "The apostles did not come down from the mountain bearing tablets of stone in their hands as did Moses, but bearing in their minds the Holy Ghost, and ministering a treasure and fountain of doctrine and of graces, they having themselves become, by divine grace, living books and codes of law."

PART V.

The Public Life of Christ.

FIRST YEAR OF HIS MINISTRY.

St. John the Baptist announces Christ.

Read carefully and study verses 19–51 *of the First Chapter of St. John's gospel.*

LESSON XCVII.

TEXT.—"And this is the testimony of John, when the Jews sent from Jerusalem priests and Levites to him, to ask him: Who art thou?" (John i. 19.)

REFLECTION.—John as a witness of Christ.

291. What urged the Jewish leaders to send an embassy to John?

The people were greatly excited by his extraordinary preaching and his remarkable virtues. His frequent reference to the kingdom of heaven as near at hand led them to suspect him to be the Messias for whom they hoped. This led them to inquire as to his character as the Messias.

292. Why did they ask him if he was Elias or the prophet?

Because they had always believed that Elias would come again before the Messias, or at least that a prophet would precede His coming.

293. What prophecy had they in mind?

That of Malachias iv. 5: "Behold, I will send you Elias the prophet, before the coming of the great and dreadful day of the Lord." And also the word of the angel, Luke i. 17: "And he shall go before Him in the spirit and power of Elias: that he may turn the hearts of the fathers unto the children, and the incredulous to the wisdom of the just, to prepare unto the Lord a perfect people."

294. How long had John been preaching when this embassy went to him?

It seems quite certain that he had been preaching and baptizing for several months, so that his fame went far and wide.

LESSON XCVIII.

TEXT.—"And he confessed, and did not deny: and he confessed: I am not the Christ. And they asked him: What then? Art thou Elias? And he said: I am not. Art thou the prophet? And he answered: No." (John i. 20, 21.)

REFLECTION.—Humility of John.

295. What was John's answer to all their questions?

He said that he was not the Messias, nor Elias, nor the prophet.

296. What did he call himself, and what did it mean?

He called himself a voice in the wilderness, because he foretold the coming of Christ, and called people to do penance as a preparation for that coming.

297. How was John a witness to Christ?

By telling the world that Christ was the Son of God, as he himself had been told by the voice of God at His baptism in the Jordan.

LESSON XCIX.

TEXT.—"The next day John saw Jesus coming to him, and he saith: Behold the Lamb of God, behold Him who taketh away the sin of the world." (John i. 29.)

REFLECTION.—Jesus our atonement.

298. When did Christ appear to John?

He appeared after His great temptation. This was Christ's first public appearance, after His trial in the desert.

299. What did John call Him, and why did he use that term?

He called Him the Lamb of God who taketh away the

sin of man. This was because He was the Paschal Lamb who was to atone for the sins of man, and a lamb was the usual offering for sin.

300. How did John know Jesus when He came to him from the desert?

He had seen the Spirit of God descend upon Him when he baptized Him in the Jordan, and he heard the voice calling Him "My beloved Son." This was evidence to him that He was the Messias, the only Son of God.

LESSON C.

TEXT.—"And Andrew the brother of Simon Peter was one of the two who had heard of John, and followed him. He findeth first his brother Simon. . . . And he brought him to Jesus. And Jesus looking upon him, said: Thou art Simon the son of Jona: thou shalt be called Cephas; which is interpreted, Peter." (John i. 40-42.)

REFLECTION.—The call of Jesus Christ.

301. Who is the second one of John's disciples, who is said to have followed Christ?

It is generally supposed to be John, the beloved disciple, the son of Zebedee and the writer of the gospel which bears his name.

302. What other disciples joined them at that time?

Simon, Philip, and Nathanael, and these, with Andrew and John, formed the first disciples of Christ.

303. Why did Nathanael hesitate?

Because, among the Jews, Nazareth at that time did not bear a very good name—in fact it was a place of reproach. Consequently he did not think it possible that the Messias could come from such a place.

The Miracle at Cana.

Read carefully and study verses 1-11 of the Second Chapter of St. John's gospel.

LESSON CI.

TEXT. — "And the third day there was a marriage in Cana of Galilee: and the Mother of Jesus was there. And Jesus also was invited, and His disciples, to the marriage." (John ii. 1, 2.)

REFLECTION.—By His presence Jesus sanctifies the family life.

304. What is meant by the "third day"?

It may refer to the time of departure from Bethabara, or the calling of Nathanael and the first disciples. By some it is thought to refer to the third day of the week, Wednesday, the day set by the Jewish law for the marriage of maidens.

305. Where had Jesus been previous to this incident, and whence did He come?

After the temptation He went to the Jordan and was recognized as the Lamb of God, selected a few disciples, journeyed north to Nazareth, and not finding His mother, came to Cana.

306. Where was Cana, and why was it called Cana of Galilee?

Cana of Galilee was a village or town not far from Capharnaum, and about four and a half miles northeast from Nazareth. There was another Cana in Aser, mentioned in Josue xix. 28, and the word Galilee is used to accurately locate the place of the miracle of Jesus. It is now known as Kefr Kenna, where a ruined church stands on the very spot of the wedding-feast.

LESSON CII.

TEXT.—"And the wine failing, the Mother of Jesus saith to Him: They have no wine. And Jesus saith to her: Woman, what is it to Me, and to thee? My hour is not yet come." (John ii. 3, 4.)

REFLECTION.—The kindness of friendship.

307. What did the failing of the wine indicate?

It is thought to indicate that the family of the wedding party was poor and humble as Jesus Himself, and the advent of the disciples made extra demands upon its hospitality.

308. Why did the Blessed Virgin precede Jesus to the marriage?

· It is supposed that as she was a close friend and perhaps a relative of the family, she went from friendship to help in the preparations for the feast.

309. Who were the disciples who accompanied Jesus?

Those whom He called to follow Him after His visit to

the Baptist; namely, Andrew, Peter, Philip, Nathanael, John, and probably James, John's brother.

LESSON CIII.

TEXT.—"His mother saith to the waiters: Whatsoever He shall say to you, do ye. Now there were set there six water-pots of stone, according to the manner of the purifying of the Jews, containing two or three measures a piece. Jesus saith to them: Fill the water-pots with water. And they filled them to the brim." (John ii. 5-7.)

REFLECTION.—Mary's influence with Jesus.

310. Was the term "Woman," as used by Jesus, a reproach?

No; the word Woman, like our English word Madam, was a form of polite address among Eastern people. In the Greek it is considered as most respectful. In the English, woman sounds harsh and reproachful, but it is not so in the original. It is not to be supposed that Jesus, the model of all virtues, would use a term of reproach to His mother.

311. How did Mary receive it and understand it?

She evidently knew that Jesus would work a miracle at her suggestion, as she immediately commanded the servants to obey Him. She certainly accepted His words, not as a reproach, but as reminding her of His submission to the divine will.

312. How did it happen that so many water-pots of stone were there?

Because of the multiplied purifications and ablutions of the Jews, whose laws bound them to the washing of the feet of guests and to the cleansing of hands frequently before all ceremonies. As this marriage at Cana was a most noteworthy one, provision was made for the many guests who had been invited.

LESSON CIV.

TEXT.—"Jesus saith to them: Fill the water-pots with water. And they filled them up to the brim. And Jesus saith to them: Draw out now, and carry to the chief steward of the feast. And they carried it. This beginning of miracles did Jesus in Cana of Galilee: and manifested His glory, and His disciples believed in Him." (John ii. 7, 8, 11.)

REFLECTION.—Great kindness of Jesus Christ.

313. Why were these stone water-pots used, rather than the wine vessels?

That it might not be said that water was merely added to the wine remaining in the vessels, and also that the quantity might silence all doubt.

314. What was the size of these water-pots?

As a measure or firkin stands for about nine gallons and the Gospel says that they held two or three measures, they must have held from eighteen to twenty-seven gallons.

315. Who was the chief steward?

He was usually a friend of the bridegroom, appointed to preside over the feast, looking after the arrangements, and tasting all wines before serving.

LESSON CV.

TEXT.—"This beginning of miracles did Jesus in Cana of Galilee: and manifested His glory, and His disciples believed in Him." (John ii. 11.)

REFLECTION.—The divine power of Christ.

316. What motives had Christ in performing this miracle?

That men, seeing His power, might be induced to believe in Him as the Son of God, with a mission of salvation to them, and that help to the neighbor in his necessities is a duty for all men.

317. What is meant by the manifesting of His glory?

It means that the power which He exercised was His own, and the glory that resulted belonged to Himself, as He was truly God.

318. What did Jesus mean when He said "My hour has not yet come"?

It may have meant either that He wished to wait until the wine had absolutely failed, or that He had intended not to manifest His divine power until He reached Jerusalem. In deference to His mother, however, He would perform the miracle when she requested it.

BIBLE TALKS.

A Jewish Marriage.

The marriage of a Jewish maiden was attended with much pomp and ceremony, the most brilliant part of which was the procession formed by the bridal couple, surrounded by the whole family. As Fouard says: "The long veil was a distinctive feature of the betrothed maiden, not only covering the head, but enwreathing the whole body and concealing from sight the white and gold-embroidered robe, her jewels, and the crown of myrtle that encircled her brow. The young maid, thus attired, awaited the bridal retinue. By her side the bridemaid kept watch with the ten virgins, who accompanied her with lamps in their hands. The bridegroom's coming is announced, and the procession, led by a troop of singers and lute and tambourine players, advanced, leading the bridegroom, gorgeously clad, his forehead wreathed with a golden turban entwined with myrtle and rose. About him march his ten friends, called 'Sons of the Groom,' holding palm-branches in their hands, while his kinsmen, acting as escort, bear lighted torches. The bridegroom and his companions enter within the dwelling of the bride, who is led by him towards the threshold, where he receives the tables of stone on which is inscribed the dowry. Then all go to the groom's house, where the banquet is held. The feast lasted for several days, and was enjoyed by all. Wine was the common drink of the people, and this was given in lavish hospitality at all marriage feasts.

Jesus at Capharnaum.

Read carefully and study verse 12 of the Second Chapter of St. John's gospel; also verse 13 of the Fourth Chapter of St. Matthew; and verse 23 of the Fourth Chapter of St. Luke.

LESSON CVI.

TEXT.—"After this He went down to Capharnaum He and His mother, and His brethren, and His disciples: and they remained there not many days." (John ii. 12.)

REFLECTION.—Fidelity to one's mission.

319. **After the marriage of Cana, whither did Jesus go?**

He returned to Nazareth, and almost immediately went

to Capharnaum, which was about the distance of a day's journey.

320. Where was Capharnaum, and what was it to be called?

It was a small city on the north shore of the Sea of Galilee, in the land of Genesareth, and was afterwards to be known as "His own city."

321. Why was it to be known as Christ's own city?

Because at His rejection by Nazareth Christ took up His abode there, and it became the scene of His greatest miracles. It was the home of the apostles Peter, Matthew, and Andrew, and also of the famous centurion who, some years before, had built its synagogue, in which Christ was later to teach.

LESSON CVII.

TEXT.—"And, leaving the city Nazareth, He came and dwelt in Capharnaum on the sea-coast, in the borders of Zabulon and of Nephthalim." (Matt. iv. 13.)

REFLECTION.—Ingratitude of Nazareth.

322. Describe the Sea of Galilee, and give the names by which it is known.

This "cither-shaped lake," as it has been called, was about fourteen miles long and six wide. It was one of the three basins filled by the waters of the Jordan on its way to the south. It was also called the Sea of Tiberias or Genesareth, or even Capharnaum, because of the towns on its banks or the country surrounding it.

323. What was the character of Capharnaum?

It was regarded as one of the most delightful places in these "Gardens of Princes," as the rabbis interpreted the meaning of Genesareth, within the confines of which it lay. It had its custom-house, synagogue, and some rich dwellings.

324. Why did Jesus visit Capharnaum at this time?
That He might thus manifest Himself in the principal town in Galilee before going to Jerusalem and beginning His ministry of preaching.

LESSON CVIII.

TEXT.—"As great things as we have heard done in Capharnaum, do also here in Thy own country." Luke iv. 23.)
REFLECTION.—Unbelief demanding a miracle.

325. How long did Christ stay in Capharnaum?
According to the Gospel narrative His first sojourn was very short, in fact it lasted but a few days. The law of the Pasch called Him to Jerusalem.

326. Did He perform any miracles during this visit?
The taunt of the Nazarenes, as related in the text from St. Luke, would lead us to infer that He did, as the renown of the miracles had spread through Galilee. They must be included in the many unrelated miracles referred to, by St. John, at the end of his gospel.

327. How did Jesus go to Jerusalem for the feast of the Pasch?
He joined company with the pilgrims in the caravans. He took the route through Perea, by way of Bethany and the Mount of Olives.

LESSON CIX.

TEXT.—"And the Pasch of the Jews was at hand, and Jesus went up to Jerusalem." (John ii. 13.)
REFLECTION.—Obedience to the law.

328. What is meant by the brethren of Jesus? Were they brothers as we understand the word?
No. Jesus was the only child of Mary, His mother, Joseph being His foster-father. Among the Jews there

were not many words expressing degrees of relationship. Hence relatives were frequently called brethren. The brethren referred to were cousins of Jesus.

329. Who were those brethren spoken of in the last lessons?

They were James the Lesser, Joseph, Simon, and Judas called Thaddeus, John, and James the Greater. Some of these were the children of Mary, wife of Cleophas or Alpheus, the sister or, as some say, cousin of the Blessed Virgin. This Mary was afterwards at the cross with the Mother of Jesus.

330. When did the journey to Jerusalem take place?

It is generally supposed to have taken place at Easter, A.D. 30, and was the beginning of Christ's second journey in the first year of His public ministry.

BIBLE TALKS.

The Bible and Tradition. (*Continued.*)

We have talked about the place which tradition holds in making known the entire truth of God, for we have seen that the Bible does not pretend to contain all the truth which God wishes men to believe. Our blessed Saviour told many things to the apostles which were never committed to writing, but which became apostolical traditions, such as the abolition of the Sabbath, the institution of Sunday as the Lord's day, the Baptism of infants, and many other points of belief upon which the Bible, as St. Augustine says, offers only conjectures. A writer has been led to say: "The apostles were the book which Jesus Christ wrote — a book written not with ink, but with the Holy Ghost." St. Matthew was the first to write a gospel, but this was not written for several years after the Ascension of Christ. Though some of the Fathers had made a list of the inspired books, the New Testament, as such, was not canonized until the Council of Hippo in 393, when it first appears as a collection of sacred writings. Tradition established its authenticity, and the Christian world so received it. The Council of Trent in 1546 reaffirmed its integrity against the attacks of the so-called Reformation. The people of God, from the beginning of their records, retained doctrines as divinely revealed which were not committed to writing. The divine worship, the existence and nature of angels, everything concerning the Redeemer, were all preserved without scriptures, first by the patriarchs in an ordinary ministry, and then by the prophets in an extraordinary ministry. Remember what Moses says in his canticle, "Remember the days of old, think upon every generation. Ask thy father and he will declare for thee; thy elders and they will tell thee." The holy man Job said, "Inquire of thy former generation and search diligently into the memory of thy fathers and they shall teach thee."

From the time of Moses the priesthood existed to interpret and convey traditions. Our blessed Saviour followed some practices which are alone warranted by tradition, and so did the Pharisees in many of their religious observances. The early Christian Church, in the words of its defenders, stands strongly for tradition. St. Irenæus, in condemning the heresy of Valentinian and Marcion, says: "But when we challenge them to that tradition which is from the apostles, which is preserved in the churches through the successions of presbyters, the heretics are averse to tradition, saying that being themselves not only wiser than presbyters, but even than apostles, they have discovered the genuine truth. Thus it turns out that, at last, they neither assent to the Scriptures nor to tradition." Origen, another teacher of the early Church, in the third century said, "That alone is to be believed to be truth which in nothing differs from the ecclesiastical and apostolical tradition;" and again, "Not to believe otherwise than as the churches of God have by succession transmitted to us." The Council of Trent says those traditions are divine which, received by the apostles from the mouth of Christ Himself, or from the apostles themselves at the dictation of the Holy Ghost, have come down even to us, transmitted, as it were, from hand to hand.

Remember that these traditions have the same authority as the Scriptures, for both are the word of God; one is called the *written word*, and the other the *unwritten word*. These traditions are found in the creeds of the Church, in the works of the Fathers, and in the decrees of Popes and councils. They are now written and found in books, but they were not written under the inspiration of the writers of the Scriptures, and are but the expressions of the living voice of the Church. Holy Scripture and Divine Tradition, as understood and interpreted by the Church, form the Catholic rule of faith.

Christ Purges the Temple.

Read carefully and study verses 13-25 of the Second Chapter of St. John's gospel, and make references to verse 14 of the Fourteenth Chapter of Exodus and verses 1-16 of the Sixteenth Chapter of Deuteronomy.

LESSON CX.

TEXT.—"And He found in the Temple them that sold oxen and sheep and doves, and the changers of money sitting." (John ii. 14.)

REFLECTION.—Irreverence in the house of God.

331. Was Jesus bound to go to the Temple? Why did He go at this time?

He was certainly not bound; but He desired by His

example to teach obedience to law. He also wished to begin His public ministry with the Jews in Jerusalem, and the Passover gave Him a great opportunity to meet them from all sections.

332. What is meant by the words "in the Temple"?
It means the outer court, or the court of the Gentiles. This court had an area of about fourteen acres, and was separated from the inner court by a high wall.

333. Why were oxen, sheep, and doves in this court as in a market-place?
For the convenience of the Jews, who were obliged by the law to offer sacrifice on feast-days. Oxen and sheep were the gifts of the rich, and doves came from the poor.

LESSON CXI.

TEXT.—"And when He had made as it were a scourge of little cords, He drove them all out of the Temple, the sheep also and the oxen, and the money of the changers He poured out, and the tables He overthrew." (John ii. 15.)

REFLECTION.—Cleansing of the soul from sin.

334. Why were money-changers in the Temple?
To make the exchange of money easy for all visitors to pay the yearly Temple tax and buy materials for the sacrifices.

335. What was the yearly Temple tax?
Half a shekel from every Jew, however poor. It was called by the law "stamped double drachma." The coin was a native one, and hence had to be purchased in Jerusalem in the Temple. It was worth about twenty-eight cents.

336. Why was Christ indignant against all this bargaining?
Because the Temple had become a market-place for

traffic. Usury and fraud resulted from the avarice of men who sought to make money by trading on the religious needs of the people.

LESSON CXII.

TEXT.—"And to them that sold doves, He said: Take these things hence, and make not the house of My Father, a house of traffic. And His disciples remembered that it was written: The zeal of Thy house hath eaten Me up." (John ii. 16, 17.)

REFLECTION.—Zeal for the house of God.

337. What did Christ do when He saw these abuses?

He took some of the flexible rushes which Orientals plat together like cords, and, twisting them into a whip, He drove out the animals and overturned the money-tables.

338. How did the people act towards Him?

They were utterly amazed, and regarded Him as a religious fanatic; still they realized that He was right in vindicating the honor of the Temple.

339. When they had recovered from their surprise, what did they ask?

They asked Jesus to show by what authority He acted thus, that they might know if He were a prophet or one sent from God.

LESSON CXIII.

TEXT.—"Jesus answered and said to them: Destroy this temple, and in three days I will raise it up. The Jews then said: Six and forty years was this Temple in building, and wilt Thou raise it up in three days? But He spoke of the temple of His body." (John ii. 19-21.)

REFLECTION.—Promise of His resurrection.

340. What did the Jews understand by these words of Christ?

They took them literally, and applied them to the

beautiful Temple in which they stood, which had been begun by Herod the Great, and which, after forty-six years, was not then entirely completed. They held this same interpretation afterwards, as we see in the accusations against Christ during His Passion.

341. What did Christ mean by the rebuilding of the temple?
He meant, as St. John says, the temple of His body, which was to be crucified and in three days afterwards would be raised from the dead again by His own power.

342. What was, then, to be the sign of Christ's authority in the world?
His resurrection from the dead, which was to prove that His mission was divine, that His doctrine was truth, and that He was indeed the Son of God and the true Messias.

Jesus and Nicodemus.

Read carefully and study verses 1-21 of the Third Chapter of St. John's gospel, and also verse 9 of the Twenty-first Chapter of Numbers.

LESSON CXIV.

TEXT.—"And there was a man of the Pharisees, named Nicodemus, a ruler of the Jews. This man came to Jesus by night, and said to Him: Rabbi, we know that Thou art come a teacher from God, for no man can do these signs which Thou dost, unless God be with him." (John iii. 1, 2.)

REFLECTION.—Earnest search after truth.

343. Who were the Pharisees, to whom Nicodemus belonged?
They were a very strict and religious sect among the

Jews. They professed a great love for the Scriptures, and lived in expectation of the Messias, who, according to their belief, was to be a great temporal prince. They despised all other Jews.

344. What is meant by the word "ruler"?

The Sanhedrim or council of seventy was composed of learned men who had great authority and respect among the Jews. They were often called rulers. Nicodemus was most probably one of these.

345. Why did he seek Jesus by night?

It is thought that he was anxious to meet Jesus and ask Him questions which would determine his faith. He was afraid of public comment, and therefore from motives of worldly prudence he chose the night that he might not be seen.

LESSON CXV.

TEXT.—"Jesus answered, and said to him: Amen, amen I say to thee, unless a man be born again, he cannot see the kingdom of God." (John iii. 3.)

REFLECTION.—The conditions of salvation.

346. What did the title rabbi signify, and to whom did it apply?

It was a title of honor and distinction and was applied to men of learning who were recognized as teachers. The Jews used it frequently in addressing Christ.

347. Why did Nicodemus assert that Jesus was a teacher from God?

Because he had seen some of His works, and he knew that only a teacher from God could perform the miracles which he witnessed, for they bore the marks of God's approbation.

348. Did not this imply a belief in Jesus as the Messias?

Not necessarily, as He might have been a prophet sent by God to announce certain truths, as had often happened in the history of the Jews. Nicodemus wanted to find out if He were such a prophet or the true Messias.

LESSON CXVI.

TEXT.—"Nicodemus saith to Him: How can a man be born when he is old? Can he enter a second time into his mother's womb and be born again?" (John iii. 4.)

REFLECTION.—The mystery of regeneration.

349. What did Jesus mean by the words "born again"?

He wanted to make Nicodemus understand the new

birth that was to become a necessary condition of salvation. As under the Jewish law a man became a child of Abraham by circumcision, so under Christ he becomes a child of God by the regeneration of Baptism.

350. How was this new birth to be effected?

By the Spirit of God, which, through the waters of Christian Baptism, was to effect a change in the hearts of believers.

351. How has the Council of Trent interpreted the words of "water and the Holy Ghost"?

It has declared that these words refer to the Sacrament of Baptism. Nicodemus, too, could have so understood them, for John the Baptist had announced that the Messias would baptize with the Holy Ghost. Thus a supernatural effect was given to the water in Baptism.

LESSON CXVII.

TEXT.—"Jesus answered: Amen, amen I say to thee, unless a man be born again of water and the Holy Ghost, he cannot enter into the kingdom of God. That which is born of the flesh, is flesh: and that which is born of the Spirit, is spirit. Nicodemus answered, and said to Him: How can these things be done?" (John iii. 5, 6, 9.)

REFLECTION.—The new birth.

352. By the words "how can these things be done" did Nicodemus express doubt in the words of Christ?

No. He no longer doubted the substance of what Christ taught, but he questioned about the way of its fulfilment.

353. What did He mean by "earthly things"?

He meant the visible things which happen on earth, and which are seen by men and yet are not believed.

354. How is the word "Spirit" interpreted, and to whom does it refer?

It is generally interpreted to mean the Holy Ghost, through whose working in the soul the new birth or regeneration is effected. As an agent He is invisible, but He produces a real effect in the soul.

LESSON CXVIII.

TEXT.—"Jesus answered, and said to him: Art thou a master in Israel, and knowest not these things? If I have spoken to you earthly things, and you believe not: how will you believe if I shall speak to you heavenly things? And as Moses lifted up the serpent in the desert; so must the Son of man be lifted up: that whosoever believeth in Him, may not perish, but may have life everlasting." (John iii. 10, 12, 14, 15.)

REFLECTION.—Salvation by the cross.

355. To what did Christ refer when He reproached Nicodemus with not knowing His meaning?

He referred to what the prophecies foretold of Christ, the Passion, and the redemption. As a master or teacher of the law, Nicodemus should have remembered the prophecies.

356. What did the reference to Moses bring to mind?

The great central truth of Christ's life, that as Moses lifted up the serpent, so that all who looked upon it might live, so Christ must be lifted up on the cross, and thus restore all men to true life.

357. Did Nicodemus follow Christ, or do we hear from him again?

It is not clear that he followed Christ then, although he is reported to have made a feeble appeal to the Sanhedrim for Him. He is not seen again until the crucifixion, when he became a stanch follower of Christ.

Jesus and the Samaritan Woman.

Read carefully and study verses 1-42 of the Fourth Chapter of St. John's gospel, and also verses 18-20 of the Twenty-third Chapter of Genesis.

LESSON CXIX.

TEXT.—"He cometh therefore to a city of Samaria which is called Sichar: near the land which Jacob gave to his son Joseph. Now Jacob's well was there. Jesus therefore being wearied with His journey, sat thus on the well. It was about the sixth hour." (John iv. 5, 6.)

REFLECTION.—Kindness to one's enemies.

358. Why did Jesus withdraw from Judea and enter Samaria?

Because of the hostility of the religious leaders, who now turned their attention from John the Baptist to Jesus.

The cleansing of the Temple and the advocacy of the new rite of Baptism caused great hatred.

359. When did all this happen in the life of Christ?
Late in December or early in January, about seven months after He began His ministry.

360. Why did Jesus go into Samaria?
The natural way to reach Galilee was through Samaria, which, though practically a part of Judea, was greatly separated from it by the mutual hatreds.

LESSON CXX.

TEXT.—"There cometh a woman of Samaria to draw water. Jesus saith to her: Give Me to drink. For His disciples were gone into the city to buy meats. Then that Samaritan woman saith to Him: How dost Thou, being a Jew, ask of me to drink, who am a Samaritan woman? For the Jews do not communicate with the Samaritans." (John iv. 7, 8, 9.)

REFLECTION.—Love of Jesus for all men.

361. Where did Jesus and His disciples rest at the time mentioned in this incident?
They rested on a low wall built around the well of Jacob. (See Genesis xxiii. 18–20.) This well was near the town of Sichar, close to the base of the mountain and near the road to Gazirim, where the Samaritans had their temple. Sichar is probably the modern Askar.

362. What were the reasons that led the Jews to hold no intercourse with the Samaritans?
The Jews were a pure race, that is, unmixed with other peoples, while the Samaritans, through intermarriage with the Assyrians, had created racial and religious antagonisms, which led to a rival temple.

363. Why did Jesus ignore all prejudices and ask the Samaritan woman for water?

He wished by this to break down these prejudices, and show at once that all men are children of God and called to salvation.

LESSON CXXI.

TEXT.—"Jesus answered, and said to her: If thou didst know the gift of God, and who He is that saith to thee, Give Me to drink: thou perhaps wouldst have asked of Him, and He would have given thee living water." (John iv. 10.)

REFLECTION.—Gift of the Spirit of God.

364. What is the "living water" which Christ offers to the Samaritan woman?

The living water of which Christ speaks refers to the Spirit of God, eternal life, symbolized by the waters of the spring, which Easterns called "living water." As water springs from an unfailing source and is fresh and overflowing, so the Spirit of God is the source of every virtue and of all good.

365. Why did she allude to Jacob, of whom she claimed to be a descendant?

She meant to say that as the well was good enough for Jacob, who according to her ideas was the greatest of men, it was good enough for his children, and she asks Christ if He has a better one. She thinks only of material good, represented by the well which she sees.

366. What did Christ mean by "true adorers"?

He meant men who worship, not by mere forms, but with true heart service. He wanted to condemn the absence of real devotion, which was manifested in servility to the letter of the law, while ignoring the spirit of it.

LESSON CXXII.

TEXT.—" Sir, I perceive that Thou art a prophet. Our fathers adored on this mountain, and You say, that at Jerusalem is the place where men must adore. Jesus saith to her: Woman believe Me, that the hour cometh, when you shall neither on this mountain, nor in Jerusalem adore the Father. But the hour cometh, and now is, when the true adorers shall adore the Father in spirit and in truth." (John iv. 19-21, 23.)

REFLECTION.—True service of God.

367. Why did this woman recognize that Jesus was a prophet?

Because He read the secret of her heart and told her of her sins, and she felt that He could know this only by divine power, although it was she who betrayed her sinfulness by coming at midday to the well, which was against the received canons of womanly modesty in those days.

368. Why did Jesus refer to her sins and thus publicly upbraid her?

In order to show that the surest way to purify the heart is to enlighten the mind. He also wished to use her as an instrument for the manifestation of His divine mission, and this she became, as her anxiety to make Him known to her people shows quite plainly.

369. What was the result of this incident on the mission of Christ?

It brought the Samaritans under His influence during the two days He spent among them, and He was recognized in their little town of Samaria as the Saviour of the world. They accepted Him in His humility, while the Jews were looking for a mighty king who was to restore Israel to the greatness of political and material power.

BIBLE TALKS.

The Catholic Church Loves the Bible.

Some people would have you believe that the Catholic Church is the enemy of the Bible, and they say that it is because she is afraid of the Bible. We know how wicked such an assertion is, because it is so untrue. Ask those people to tell you from whom they received whatever they have of the Bible to-day. Is it not from the Catholic Church? Bible Christianity, as it is called, did not come into existence until the sixteenth century, and took as the book which was to give it its religious forms the very book which the Catholic Church for fifteen centuries before had preserved and defended. She was the only witness in the world to the fact that the saints and doctors of the Christian Church had kept the Bible from being destroyed or mutilated. The Catholic Church has carefully guarded the treasure of the word of God and jealously watched over every line in it. Her doctors and scholars have been urged to a life of labor in determining its genuine readings and in making its sense clear. Volume on volume, in every language under the sun, has been written by them to make known its value and its authentic character. In days of persecution her children were threatened with direct punishment for abandoning any one of the sacred books to the infidel. The decrees of her councils from Laodicea to the Vatican have determined the authenticity and the genuineness of the sacred text. Her monks and nuns, her priests and religious, have been obliged to recite from it daily in the holy office; her preachers have been forced to explain it to the people, and every doctrine in her code must find its basis in the Bible text. Is this evidence of love or hate? See all through the ages how she has defended the text against the base passions of men who would mutilate it or change its meaning to suit their lives.

It was her St. Jerome who, at the command of Pope Damasus, undertook to translate the Bible into the Latin, and gave us what is known as the Vulgate. The Catholic Church has always stood against the abuse of the Bible, and she has demanded that with her seal the book be stamped with her authority, the same seal without which so great a genius as St. Augustine said he would have rejected the four gospels. It was her spirit that made so many saints read it with uncovered head and on bended knees, so deep was their veneration for the word of God. Father Faber expresses the thought of the Church beautifully when he says: "The holy book lies like a bunch of myrrh in the bosom of the Church, a power for sanctification, like to which in kind and degree there is no other except the sacraments of the precious blood." Too many people are willing to give the Bible to non-Catholics as if it belonged to them. Remember if it were not for the Catholic Church, which is the true Church of Christ, there would be no Bible in the world. She received it from the apostles, she preserved it for mankind, she finds in it one of the remote rules of faith and morals, and she loves the Bible because she loves Jesus Christ, Our Saviour.

Healing of the Nobleman's Son.

Read carefully and study verses 46-54 of the Fourth Chapter of St. John's gospel.

LESSON CXXIII.

TEXT.—" And there was a certain ruler whose son was sick at Capharnaum. He having heard that Jesus was come from Judea into Galilee, went to Him, and prayed Him to come down and heal his son: for he was at the point of death." (John iv. 46, 47.)

REFLECTION.—Confidence in God.

370. Who was the ruler spoken of in this narrative, and what was his character?

He was one of the military or civil officers of Herod Antipas, who was commonly called king. By some he is thought to be Manahew, the son of Herod's nurse, and by others Chusa, Herod's intendant, whose wife afterwards gratefully ministered to Christ. He was a man of authority, and bore an excellent character.

371. How did he hear of Christ, and why did he come to Him to cure his son?

The name and fame of Christ as a prophet and more than a prophet had so spread among the people, even among those at the royal court, that the ruler was led to trust in His divine power to restore his son to health, for he knew of the miracles already performed. He was in despair of all other means and resolved to ask Him to cure his child.

372. How did Jesus receive him, and what did He do?

He received him with kindness and pity, for He realized the great faith which he possessed. He determined to teach a lesson as well as to perform a miracle, and hence He dwelt upon the idea that He was not merely a miracle-worker, but the Redeemer.

LESSON CXXIV.

TEXT.—"Jesus therefore said to him: Unless you see signs and wonders you believe not. The ruler saith to him: Lord, come down before that my son die. Jesus saith to him: Go thy way, thy son liveth. The man believed the word which Jesus said to him, and went his way." (John iv. 48-50.)

REFLECTION.—Perseverance in prayer.

373. Why did Christ utter this reproach, and what bearing did it have on the miracle?

To show that it was not necessary for Him to go to Capharnaum, as His will alone would have been sufficient. Christ did not reproach the ruler for asking that a miracle be performed, but He wished him to understand that, as He was God, His power was divine and could be exercised even at a distance. But we may easily believe that the crowd which gathered wished for a visible proof of the miracle.

374. What effect had Christ's words on the ruler?

As soon as He spoke the words "thy son liveth" the ruler believed in His word and hence had faith in Him, for he was convinced that Christ was God, and that His word was enough to bring back to health the boy that was sick.

375. What was the character of his faith, and should we strive to possess it?

It had the characteristic of true faith, for he believed without seeing. He seemed possessed of the idea that Christ was God, and, since God had spoken, that was enough. There was no longer any doubt, and he went away satisfied that his son lived. Notice the ruler first believed in Christ's word and then believed in Christ Himself. If we would have faith pleasing to God we should believe as the ruler did. Faith knows neither doubt nor hesitation; it is absolute.

LESSON CXXV.

TEXT.—"And as he was going down, his servants met him: and they brought word, saying, that his son lived. He asked therefore of them the hour, wherein he grew better. And they said to him: Yesterday at the seventh hour the fever left him." (John iv. 51, 52.)

REFLECTION.—God's goodness to the ruler.

376. Where did this miracle take place, and how far was it from Capharnaum?

The word of Jesus was said at Cana, in Galilee, where the miracle of the wedding-feast had taken place. It was about twenty-eight miles from Capharnaum, where the ruler dwelt. As it took nearly a day to make the journey, it is probable that the ruler did not reach home until late that evening or early next morning. He was confident of finding his son entirely cured, as a result of his faith in Christ and Christ's word to him.

377. What is meant by "the seventh hour," and how does it correspond with our time?

As St. John computed time, it was the seventh hour from sunrise, which occurred about six o'clock in the morning. It would correspond, in our computation, to one o'clock in the afternoon.

378. What was the Jewish method for computing time?

The Jews had the custom of computing time by beginning the legal day of twenty-four hours at sunset, and thus their day was from evening to evening. After the captivity, while they still held to this method, they also followed the Chaldeans, who computed from sunrise to sunrise as a legal day. St. John followed the latter.

LESSON CXXVI.

TEXT.—"The father therefore knew that it was at the same hour, that Jesus said to him: Thy son liveth: and himself believed and his whole house. This is again the second miracle that Jesus did, when He was come out of Judea into Galilee." (John iv. 53, 54.)

REFLECTION.—Gratitude for God's favors.

379. What effect had this miracle upon the ruler and his family?

It confirmed him in his belief that his faith in Christ was well founded, and that He was indeed the Messias, and he and his family believed and became followers of Christ.

380. Why does St. John use the word "second," as Christ had performed many miracles?

It may be to recall the fact of the first miracle at Cana at the wedding-feast, and to urge this one as equally important. It was the second in Cana, and not second in the order of miracles.

381. Whither did Jesus go after this miracle, and why?

It is probable that Jesus did not stay long in Cana. He then went to Nazareth, where the fame of His miracles had preceded Him. He entered the synagogue where he had worshipped as a boy, and there He taught that the Scriptures were fulfilled in Him. The Jews were indignant at His words, and expelled Him from the synagogue and threatened to throw Him from the summit of a neighboring hill. But He passed through them and went His way. He then went to Capharnaum, where He was destined to exercise much of His public ministry, to call the apostles, and to organize His work.

Jesus at Nazareth.

Read carefully and study verses 14-30 of the Fourth Chapter of St. Luke's gospel.

LESSON CXXVII.

TEXT.—"And Jesus returned in the power of the Spirit into Galilee, and the fame of Him went out through the whole country. And He taught in their synagogues, and was magnified by all. And He came to Nazareth where He was brought up: and He went into the synagogue according to His custom on the Sabbath-day, and He rose up to read." (Luke iv. 14-16.)

REFLECTION.—Fidelity to religion.

382. Why did Christ enter the synagogues, and especially that of Nazareth?

That He might verify the prophecies and teach the true religion, for they were the meeting-places of the Jews for religious services. As a boy He went to the one in Nazareth, and hence was familiar with it as the place where He worshipped.

383. Why is it said of Him that He stood up?

It was customary to stand up while reading the Scriptures and to sit down while explaining them. His distinction, no doubt, led them that day to invite Him to conduct the services.

384. What did the services, as such, consist of?

They consisted of a certain liturgical form of prayers to which the people responded. Psalms were sung, the law and the prophecies were read, an address followed, after which the services closed by a prayer. These exercises did not demand a priest, and any prominent man was allowed to conduct them.

LESSON CXXVIII.

TEXT.—"And the book of Isaias the prophet was delivered unto Him. And as He unfolded the book, He found the place where it was written: *The Spirit of the Lord is upon me; wherefore He hath anointed me, to preach the Gospel to the poor He hath sent me, to heal the contrite of heart.*" (Luke iv. 17, 18.)

REFLECTION.—Mission of Christ.

385. What was the book which was delivered to Christ in the synagogue?

It was in the form of a parchment roll, containing the prophecies of Isaias, and was taken from the sacred box, placed behind the pulpit, where the sacred books were kept.

386. What is meant by "He found the place"?

It means the passage in Isaias which He wished to use as a text for His sermon that He might show the fulfilment of the prophecy.

387. To whom did the prophet refer in this quotation from Isaias lxi. 1, 2?

It was to Christ, who was filled with the Spirit of God, who influenced and guided Him, who was in very deed the Word of God.

LESSON CXXIX.

TEXT.—" And when He had folded the book, He restored it to the minister, and sat down. And the eyes of all in the synagogue were fixed on Him. And He began to say to them: This day is fulfilled this scripture in your ears. . . . And they wondered at the words of grace that proceeded from His mouth, and they said: Is not this the son of Joseph?" (Luke iv. 20–22.)

REFLECTION.—Christ the fulfilment of God's promise.

388. Who was the subject of this first great discourse of Christ?

He Himself was the subject. To make Himself known was the object of His life, and hence from the very beginning of His public ministry He forced Himself upon His hearers that all might know the object of His mission and the authority which He possessed.

389. What was the keynote of Christ's first discourse?

Love for the poor, to whom He was sent as an anointed one to evangelize them; love for those in sorrow that He might heal their wounds; love to the blind that they might by Him be made to see.

390. What was meant by the acceptable year?

It meant the time when God was to visit His people with His choicest blessings. That year was also jubilee year, which was always regarded as a type of the time of the Messias. Hence it was a fitting time to proclaim Himself the Saviour.

LESSON CXXX.

Text.—" And all they in the synagogue, hearing these things, were filled with anger. And they rose up and thrust Him out of the city: and they brought Him to the brow of the hill, whereon their city was built, that they might cast Him down headlong. But He passing through the midst of them, went His way." (Luke iv. 28–30.)

Reflection.—Ingratitude of men.

391. How was it that they did not see the fulfilment of prophecy in Christ?

They saw the man only in Him whom they knew as a boy in Nazareth, watched over by Joseph, the carpenter; and they could not realize that out of such common surroundings could come that great king whom they looked for in the Messias.

392. Why were they so suddenly incensed against Him?

Because they foolishly thought that He considered them as no better than Gentiles and lepers, and, being Nazarenes like Himself, they could not bear to have Him thus speak to them. Their pride was wounded and their ambition thwarted.

393. In their anger what did they do?

They interrupted the service and thrust Jesus out of the synagogue, and would have done Him violence were it not that He passed through them and went His way.

394. Why did He select Capharnaum for His residence?

He had previously visited it and experienced its kindness. It was also an important town on the Lake of Galilee, and thus became a great centre for missionary work in His Galilean ministry.

SECOND YEAR OF CHRIST'S MINISTRY.

Christ's First Disciples.

Read carefully and study verses 1-11 of the Fifth Chapter of St. Luke's gospel; also verses 18-22 of the Fourth Chapter of St. Matthew's gospel.

LESSON CXXXI.

TEXT.—"And it came to pass, that when the multitudes pressed upon Him to hear the word of God, He stood by the Lake of Genesareth. And saw two ships standing by the lake: but the fishermen were gone out of them and were washing their nets." (Luke v. 1, 2.)

REFLECTION.—Nearness of the kingdom of God.

395. Why was this lake called the Lake of Genesareth?

Because of the land by that name, on its western side, which in the time of Christ was densely populated. It was also called the Lake of Galilee. It was sometimes called Tiberias because of the city of that name on its borders, and by this name it is known at the present time.

396. Where is this lake located, and what are its dimensions?

It is in Galilee, whence, according to some of the Evangelists, it took its name. It is formed by the river Jordan, and is thirteen miles long and six miles broad, located among the mountains, and was said to be one of the seven seas of Chanaan, which God reserved for Himself.

397. Why was it selected as the scene of so much of Christ's labors?

Because it was the most thickly populated and prosperous section of Palestine, and the people had already manifested great interest in Him and in His teachings.

LESSON CXXXII.

TEXT.—" And going up into one of the ships that was Simon's, He desired him to draw back a little from the land. And sitting He taught the multitudes out of the ship. Now when He had ceased to speak, He said to Simon: Launch out into the deep, and let down your nets for a draught." (Luke v. 3, 4.)

REFLECTION.—Christ's choice of Peter.

398. Who were the fishermen with whom Christ came in contact in this incident?

Simon, afterwards called Peter, Andrew, James, and John, whom He had known for some time previously, and who had shown a willingness to be His disciples.

399. Had the fact of entering Simon's bark any special significance?

It would seem so, and it is generally accepted that by this act Christ manifested His confidence in Simon Peter and His intention to make him the head of His apostles and of His Church.

400. Why did He cause them to draw back from the land?

That He might the better address the crowd who gathered on the bank, many of whom found seats upon the basaltic columns, that were piled upon the shore. He sat down, that He might maintain the usual posture of the teacher.

LESSON CXXXIII.

TEXT.—"And Simon answering, said to Him: Master, we have labored all the night, and have taken nothing: but at Thy word I will let down the net. And when they had done this, they enclosed a very great multitude of fishes, and their net broke." (Luke v. 5, 6.)

REFLECTION.—Reward of obedience.

401. Why did the apostle speak of the night as a time of labor?

Because the night was regarded as the best time for a certain class of fish, and hence they were not encouraged to hope for much in the fulness of the daytime.

402. Was the apostle's act one of doubt or discouragement?

It was neither. It was full of faith, as he expressed it when he said "at Thy word." He knew Christ, and had seen Him perform miracles at Cana, and might easily have expected a miracle, if need be, to illustrate the power of the Messias.

LESSON CXXXIV.

Text.—" Which when Simon Peter saw, he fell down at Jesus's knees, saying: Depart from me, for I am a sinful man, O Lord. For he was wholly astonished, and all that were with him, at the draught of the fishes which they had taken." (Luke v. 8, 9.)

Reflection.—Man's unworthiness.

403. How did Simon Peter regard this draught of fishes which nearly caused the sinking of the boats?

He regarded it as another manifestation of God's power and goodness, through the miracle performed by Christ. He was a careful fisherman, and could estimate the ordinary results of the men's work.

404. Why does Christ call Simon by a fuller name than before?

Because this moment marks an event in the apostle's life. Hereafter he is to be known as Peter, rather than Simon, for Christ has a great mission awaiting this earnest, faithful, simple fisherman. It is to be the head of His Church and His first vicar on earth.

405. Why did Simon Peter call on Christ to depart from him?

He simply asserted his unworthiness to be near such divine power. It was an expression of humility, when he realized his diffidence in casting out his nets and his general idea of the great distance between the Creator and creatures.

LESSON CXXXV.

Text.—" And so were also James and John the sons of Zebedee, who were Simon's partners. And Jesus saith to Simon: Fear not: from henceforth thou shalt catch men. And having brought their ships to land, leaving all things they followed Him." (Luke v. 10, 11.)

Reflection.—The apostolic spirit.

406. What did Christ mean by the words "thou shalt catch men"?

He meant that henceforth they would be fishers of men, catching them in the nets of the Gospel. Christ draws men to Him by the things with which they are familiar. He gave a star to lead the Magi, and a fish to draw the fishermen.

407. What are we to understand by the words "leaving all things"?

We are to understand that these fishermen recognized in this incident a call from God to abandon all worldly pursuits and business and become the followers of Jesus Christ. They left their nets and boats, and ever afterwards went with Christ.

408. What was the result of this act of the fishermen?

It resulted in their being called to be apostles, who were to be taught by Christ Himself what to believe and what to teach and do. It shows to us all what we should be willing to sacrifice for Christ and the Gospel.

BIBLE TALKS.

The Catholic Church Preserved the Bible.

So much has been said of late years by the enemies of the Catholic Church concerning the Bible that one might be falsely led to suspect that the Bible was not fully known until the Reformation, something over three centuries ago. They would have you believe that the Bible was really lost and never would have been brought into use again, if they had not discovered its hiding-place and brought it into the daylight where all might see and read it. How false all such charges are against the one Church which has preserved the Bible for all the ages! We saw, in our last Talk, how the Church loved it during the fifteen hundred years that passed from the days of the apostles until the Reformers abandoned the Church and set up a religion of their own, which they attempted to build upon a private interpretation of the Bible. During all that time the Church constantly watched over the sacred text and preserved it, and had it carefully translated into a hundred different languages: and all this before the invention of printing. Her martyrs gave up their lives in the persecution of Diocletian rather than yield one of the sacred books, and in the wars with the barbarians her monks fled to the mountains with the books, or hid them in safe places, lest a single word be lost. The so-called Reformers received the Bible from the Catholic Church, built their religious forms upon it alone, and then said she had corrupted it and was corrupt herself. Christ had promised that His Church should never fail, and the Bible says so; and yet they would have us believe that she not only failed, but that she poisoned the fountains of truth in corrupting the Scriptures. Who alone can give you now a satisfactory and consistent account of the Bible from the beginning, from the first century to the sixteenth, and on down to the present time? The Catholic Church and the Catholic Church only. By her authority she defined what constituted the Bible, explained its meaning, proving clearly from that that it was to her that Christ said: "Go teach all nations." This led St. Augustine to exclaim: "I would not believe the Gospel if the authority of the Church did not move me to do so." Men rebelled against her at different times, used the Bible against her, but to them all she quoted the very words of Our Saviour: "Search the Scriptures, for in them you think you have eternal life, and they are they that testify of Me."

See what her great saints said of the Bible. St. Clement of Rome in the first century: "They are the oracles of the Holy Ghost and can contain nothing unjust or false." St. Irenaeus: "Perfect, because the word of God and His Spirit speaks in them." St. Athanasius: "All over, the Scriptures, whether new or old, have proceeded from divine inspiration." St. Augustine styles the Scriptures "the epistle of the Almighty to His creatures." St. Gregory the Great, who was one of the Popes, speaking of the Book of Job, says: "Who wrote these things is a very superfluous question, since it is faithfully believed that the Holy Ghost is the author of the book. He, therefore, wrote these things who dictated them to the writer. He wrote them who was the inspiration of the work, and who by the voice of the writer has written them for us." Pope Eugenius IV. said to the Council of Florence that the Bible should be received: "Since by the inspiration of the same spirit the holy men of both Testaments have spoken, whose books, contained under the following titles, the Church receives and venerates." This great Council had no discussion upon the canon of Scripture, showing that the Latin and Greek churches were one in belief about it.

This shows that the scholars, saints, and Councils of the Catholic Church venerated the Scriptures and expressed the thought of the Church. Why should she not venerate the Scriptures, since they were given in her charge, and by her children they were preserved and kept intact? Her saints were nourished by them and her altars have a place of honor for them.

The Call of St. Matthew.

Read carefully and study verses 9-15 of the Ninth Chapter of St. Matthew's gospel.

LESSON CXXXVI.

Text.—" And when Jesus passed on from thence, He saw a man sitting in the custom-house, named Matthew ; and He saith to him: Follow Me. And he arose up, and followed Him." (Matt. ix. 9.)

Reflection.—Obedience to the call of God.

409. What was the name by which Matthew was known?

He was known as Levi, and as such he is named in the gospels of St. Mark and St. Luke. He was the son of Alpheus, and was named Matthew by Christ, which signifies "gift of God," in order probably to blot out all recollection of his former life. In his own gospel he is called Matthew, and no reference is made to his former name.

410. What was his occupation, and how was it regarded among the Jews?

He was a collector of government taxes for the Romans, and all such were detested because of their office and their odious practices. They were excommunicated as apostates and Gentiles, and classed among sinners.

411. Where was the tax-booth of Matthew located?

At Capharnaum, on the great Roman highway which led from Damascus by the northern side of the Sea of Galilee, near the plain of Genesareth. Christ was obliged to pass by it whenever He went along that road.

LESSON CXXXVII.

Text.—" And it came to pass as He was sitting at meat in the house, behold many publicans and sinners came, and sat down with Jesus and His disciples." (Matt. ix. 10.)

Reflection.—Jesus, Saviour of all.

412. Where were these tax-collectors stationed, and how did they perform their office?

The Romans had established tax-booths at the foot of the mountains, by the seaside, and on the great highways, near the entrance to bridges, and close to the mouths of the rivers, that all people passing might be obliged to pay the tax. This was exacted oftentimes with great severity and injustice, and thus the publicans enriched themselves by their exorbitance.

413. How was it that Matthew accepted the invitation of Jesus so promptly?

It is probable that he became a believer in Him long before this, so that when Jesus called him to abandon his business and become His disciple he was prepared to do so, having experienced a change of heart by corresponding to divine grace so freely given.

414. How was it that he invited Christ to a feast?

As Simon invited the Saviour to a feast after his call to the apostolate, so did Matthew, that thus the Master might become the guest of His disciples. He also desired his friends to meet the Saviour and listen to His teaching, in hopes that they might be converted from their ways.

LESSON CXXXVIII.

TEXT.—"And the Pharisees seeing it, said to His disciples: Why doth your Master eat with publicans and sinners? But Jesus hearing it, said: They that are in health need not a physician, but they that are ill." (Matt. ix. 11, 12.)

REFLECTION.—All men called to salvation.

415. Why did the Pharisees go to the disciples rather than to Christ with their complaint?

Probably because they were so overawed by His miracles that they did not wish to have an open rupture with Him, yet they wished to protest against His association with publicans and sinners, which their customs had led them to consider as forbidden.

416. Why did Jesus give answer to their complaint?
To show the true idea of redemption and to strengthen His disciples, who might have been weakened in their confidence by such reference to Jewish prejudices and customs.

417. What was meant by the words "They that are in health need not a physician"?
They were used to express a very plain truth—that Christ came to save sinners, who, because of sin which affects the soul, need the divine Physician to act as a healer. These words also suggest to the Pharisees the hollowness of their pretence that they were in spiritual health or free from sin.

LESSON CXXXIX.

TEXT.—"Then came to Him the disciples of John, saying: Why do we and the Pharisees fast often: but Thy disciples do not fast? And Jesus said to them: Can the children of the bridegroom mourn, as long as the bridegroom is with them? But the days will come when the bridegroom shall be taken away from them: and then they shall fast." (Matt. ix. 14, 15.)

REFLECTION.—Christ's prediction of His Passion.

418. How often did the Pharisees fast, and why was this question raised?
There was the great fast of the day of atonement, prescribed by the law; but besides that they voluntarily fasted twice a week—on Mondays and Thursdays. Some think that Matthew's feast occurred on a Monday, one of the days of fasting, and consequently scandal arose.

419. Who was the "bridegroom" to whom Jesus referred?

The bridegroom to whom He referred was Christ Himself, as John the Baptist had called Him by that name. He had come to lead home His bride, which was the synagogue. All the disciples of Jesus were, therefore, friends of the bridegroom, and, according to Jewish custom, would be invited to the marriage-feast, and would be called friends of the bridechamber.

420. To what did Jesus allude when He spoke of the bridegroom being taken away?

He alluded to the days of His Passion, when gloom would come to the disciples, and sorrow and fasting would be called for. Then fasting would have a real meaning, for sorrow and fasting have a certain kinship and usually go together. Hence the Church has the Lenten fast, because of the Passion of Christ and as a preparation for the future joy of the Easter days.

BIBLE TALKS.

The Dead Sea.

This sea is known in the Bible as the Salt Sea, or the Sea of the Plain, and also the Sea of Sodom. The Greeks and Latins called it the Dead Sea. It is the third and last lake found in the course of the Jordan from the Lebanon Mountains to the Gulf of Akaba. It receives the waters of the Jordan. Smith in his Dictionary of the Bible says: "It is of an oblong form, of tolerably regular contour, interrupted only by a large and long peninsula which projects from the eastern shore, near its southern end, and virtually divides the expanse of water into two portions, connected by a long, narrow, and somewhat devious passage." Its greatest width is 10½ miles, its length 4 miles; it is 1300 feet below the level of the Mediterranean Sea, and in some places it is 1300 feet deep. It is well to remember that the Dead Sea now covers the valley that Lot chose for his abode.

The Call of the Twelve Apostles.

Read carefully and study verses 12-16 of the Sixth Chapter of St. Luke's gospel. Read also verses 13-19 of the Third Chapter of St. Mark's gospel and verses 2-4 of the Tenth Chapter of St. Matthew's gospel.

LESSON CXL.

Text.—"And it came to pass in those days, that He went out into a mountain to pray, and He passed the whole night in the prayer of God." (Luke vi. 12.)

Reflection.—Prayer as a preparation for important acts.

421. When did this event take place?

In the middle of the second year of the ministry of Christ, some time in the midsummer of the year 28.

422. What mountain is referred to in these words of St. Luke?

It is commonly believed to have been the Mount of the Beatitudes, or, as it is known in Bible geography, the Horns of Hattin, so called from the village of Hattin, located near its base, on the western coast of the Sea of Galilee.

423. Why did Jesus pass the night in prayer?

That He might teach us to prepare for grave events by earnest prayer. He did not need it, but He did it to give us an example.

LESSON CXLI.

Text.—"And going up into a mountain, He called unto Him whom He would Himself: and they came to Him. And He made that twelve should be with Him." (Mark iii. 13, 14.)

Reflection.—Divine vocation.

424. What is meant by the words "whom He would Himself"?

It means that the call of the twelve to the apostleship was gratuitous and came wholly from Jesus Christ. He alone chose them from among all the disciples and made them His apostles.

425. Had He made any choice of any of them before this moment?

Yes, five at least, and perhaps seven, were spoken to about the apostolate some time before, as we may see by consulting Mark i. 16–20 and John i. 43, 45; but the choice recorded now was final and formal.

426. What was the object of their apostolate as mentioned by St. Mark?

That they might be with Him as companions and helpers, to be trained by Him in His truths, and to fulfil His mission for the establishment of His Church.

LESSON CXLII.

Text.—" And that He might send them to preach. And He gave them power to heal sicknesses, and to cast out devils." (Mark iii. 14, 15.)

Reflection.—Power of God given to men.

427. What was the mission of the apostles?

To go forth and teach nations, preaching the Gospel of Christ and exercising His ministry among men. They were to take His place and build up a visible Church, which was to continue His work forever.

428. Why were they called apostles?

Because Christ wished to impress upon them the importance of the message He was afterwards to give them, when He would send them as messengers of His Gospel. They are now called to be apostles, but after the Resurrection He will constitute them apostles.

429. What is the significance of the number twelve?

As there were twelve tribes of Israel whose names were written on the twelve gates of the New Jerusalem, so would the names of the twelve apostles be found on the twelve foundation-stones of His Church.

LESSON CXLIII.

Text.—" And to Simon He gave the name Peter: and James the son of Zebedee, and John the brother of James, and He named them Boanerges, which is the Sons of Thunder: and Andrew and Philip, and Bartholomew and Matthew, and Thomas and James of Alpheus, and Thaddeus, and Simon the Cananean, and Judas Iscariot, who also betrayed Him." (Mark iii. 16-19.)

Reflection.—The agency of men in religion.

430. How many lists of the apostles have we, and what is noted about them?

There are four lists, which are found in St. Matthew,

St. Mark, St. Luke, and the Acts of the Apostles. It is to be noted that Peter is named first in them all, thus indicating priority of rank.

431. What is there of significance in the change of Simon's name to Peter?

It shows the intention of Christ to give him special powers or a special work, just as God did in the Old Testament with Abraham and Sara. Peter means rock, which was to signify the founding of the Church upon him.

432. What were the characteristics of the apostles?

They were plain, simple men, mostly fishermen, without much education or means, and free from much of the errors or evils of the day. They were all Galileans except Judas, who was from Karioth in Judea.

The Sermon on the Mount.

Read carefully and study verses 1-48 of the Fifth Chapter of St. Matthew's gospel and verses 20-49 of the Sixth Chapter of St. Luke's gospel.

LESSON CXLIV.

TEXT.—"And Jesus seeing the multitudes, went up into a mountain, and when He was sat down, His disciples came unto Him, and opening His mouth, He taught them, saying: Blessed are the poor in spirit: for theirs is the kingdom of heaven. Blessed are they that suffer persecution for justice' sake: for theirs is the kingdom of heaven." (Matt. v. 1, 2, 3, 10.)

433. Why is this first great discourse of Christ called the Sermon on the Mount?

Because it was delivered on the mountain known as the Horns of Hattin, whither Christ had retired for prayer. The mountain was afterwards to be called the Mount of

Beatitudes, because of the opening sentences of Christ's great discourse. The hillsides were covered with people, and the apostles were close to Christ.

434. Why are the opening sentences called Beatitudes?

Because of the promise of blessedness which is made to those who practise the virtue of which Christ speaks. They are the conditions for entering the kingdom of heaven.

435. What are the main divisions of this discourse?

(1) The conditions of membership in the kingdom of Christ; (2) the duties of Christ's subjects to the world in which they live; (3) the relations of this doctrine with the Old Law and the Pharisees; (4) rules for Christian life.

LESSON CXLV.

TEXT.—"You are the salt of the earth, but if the salt lose its savor, wherewith shall it be salted ? it is good for nothing any more but to be cast out and to be trodden on by men. You are the light of the world. A city seated on a mountain cannot be hid." (Matt. v. 13, 14.)

REFLECTION.—The influence of a good Christian life.

436. What is meant by this reference to salt ?

It means that as salt preserves food from corruption and helps it to keep its taste, so virtue seasons and preserves life; for without virtue life is worthless. So the Christians, and especially the apostles, are called to be the very salt of the earth, and their lives should be examples of all goodness to the world.

437. What are we to understand by the words "the light of the world" ?

We may understand them to mean a good life, which, in the moral world, can be likened to the sun in the material world. Christ calls Himself the Light of the world in John viii. 12, and all are called to be like Him. This is true of all Christians, but in a most special manner it is true of His apostles and ministers, who are called to be a light illumining the pathway of all men.

438. Which is the city on the hill, which cannot be hid ?

Some think it refers to Jerusalem, while others think it refers to lofty Safed, which could be seen from the spot where Jesus stood. It may also be considered as an example of the prominence of a good Christian life which may be seen by all. The Church of Christ is represented as the city on the mountain to be seen by men in all time.

LESSON CXLVI.

TEXT.—"You have heard that it hath been said: Thou shalt love thy neighbor, and hate thy enemy. But I say to you: Love your enemies, do good to them that hate you: and pray for them that persecute and calumniate you: that you may be the children of your Father who is in heaven." (Matt. v. 43, 44.)

REFLECTION.—Law of love.

439. Who had said that men should hate their enemies?

This had been said by the Pharisees, who desired to establish a greater separation between the Jews and the Gentiles, and was based on what Moses did to guard against private revenge. The Pharisees also wished to have their followers believe that "an eye for an eye and a tooth for a tooth" was good doctrine to follow.

440. To whom does Christ refer, in a special manner, when He uses the word "enemies"?

He referred to those whom the Jews regarded as their enemies. As the Jews understood the word, it meant all who were not of the chosen race of Israel, as well as those who did injury to them among themselves. The Samaritans were in a special manner subjected to the enmity of the Jews. To insist that these should be objects of love was to emphasize in the strongest manner possible the new law of Christian love.

441. What do you understand by the allusion to the necessity of being children of the heavenly Father?

Christ wishes to have them understand that if they desire to be children of God they must have that love which He has for all men, and thus they must act like God Himself, who sheds the blessings of nature upon His enemies as well as upon His friends. Christ also was to die for all, even for those who put Him to death.

LESSON CXLVII.

TEXT.—"Thus therefore shall you pray: Our Father who art in heaven, hallowed be Thy name. Thy kingdom come. Thy will be done on earth as it is in heaven. Give us this day our supersubstantial bread. And forgive us our debts, as we also forgive our debtors. And lead us not into temptation. But deliver us from evil. Amen." (Matt. vi. 9-13.)

REFLECTION.—Prayer taught by Christ.

442. What is the first part of this prayer of Our Lord?

The opening words, "Our Father who art in heaven," indicate the address to God to whom we pray, and who by His grace has adopted us as His children and hence is our Father. The word "our" shows our relations to our brethren, while "heaven" marks our Father's home and our home.

443. How many petitions are in the "Our Father," and to what do they refer?

There are seven petitions in it, the first three of which refer to the glory of God, and the last four to our spiritual wants that we may obtain salvation.

444. How may you explain that this constitutes a perfect prayer?

God is addressed as a Father on whose love we depend that He may be ever honored, loved, and obeyed. Having proclaimed His glory, we petition for our needs, and pray for the grace to do our duty and keep from sin.

BIBLE TALKS.

The Bible and the People.

Sometimes you will hear it said that the Catholic Church is not willing to allow the people to read the Bible. This is not the worst thing they say, for they add that the Church has done this in order to keep the people in ignorance of the truth. How wicked such statements are may be seen from what we have already said about the Bible. Besides that, are you not studying the Bible now in your classes? Are you not encouraged to study it more, with the promise of reward for faithful work? Has not our Holy Father, Leo XIII., written a letter lately in which any one who reads may see his intense desire to have Catholics study the Bible? Still we must remember that the Bible is not so absolutely necessary to our faith as it is to non-Catholics, for we regard the Bible as one of the two remote rules of faith in which we find the greater part of our doctrines; but our proximate rule of faith, that is our teacher, is the Church established by Christ to interpret the Bible and tradition. The man who has no religion except as he picks it out of the Bible, and no teacher except the Bible as he reads it, must necessarily need the Bible all the time. The Catholic Church received the care of the divine books, and was appointed the interpreter of them; and this has made the Church extremely jealous not only of every book of the Bible, but of every word as well, in the original and also in the translations into different languages. In the Old Law the Bible or Old Testament was carefully kept within the golden ark and explained by the masters of the synagogues.

When Christ came and built His Church, He transferred to her the care of the Scriptures not only of the Old Law, but of the New, and commissioned the priesthood of His Church to explain them to the people; and this has been done in every age and in every language under the sun. In the early ages books were scarce, and consequently very valuable, and a Bible was reputed worth its weight in gold. Every word in it had to be written by the patient scribes whose lives were spent in preserving all that was good in literature and religion. In the thirteenth century false teachers arose in France, who mutilated the sacred text and preached unholy doctrines, for which they falsely asserted the authority of the Bible. To protect the people from this poison of error, the Council of Toulouse, in 1229, forbade laymen to read the Bible except by the permission of the bishop. This law was local, and simply a measure of protection. Later, when St. Dominic destroyed the Albigensian heresy and converted the heretics, this prohibition ceased.

Again, when the private-judgment theory of Protestantism, in the sixteenth century, struck a blow at the integrity of the Bible, and many books which had always been received as sacred were declared by the sectaries to be non-inspired, the Church, in the Council of Trent, passed a decree prohibiting any one to print the Bible without a special license, or any layman to read it without a special permit from the bishop. Again, this was a measure of protection by which the poor people might be guarded against the mutilated or changed word of Scripture. In 1757, in the time of Pope Benedict XIV., the laws were modified, and versions of the Bible approved by the Holy See or from learned Catholics were permitted. Any layman could then read any authorized version.

THIRD YEAR OF CHRIST'S MINISTRY.

Multiplication of the Loaves and Fishes.

Read carefully and study verses 30-44 of the Sixth Chapter of St. Mark; verses 13-21 of the Fourteenth Chapter of St. Matthew, 10-17 of the Ninth Chapter of St. Luke, and 1-14 of the Sixth Chapter of St. John.

LESSON CXLVIII.

TEXT.—"And Jesus going out saw a great multitude: and He had compassion on them, because they were as sheep not having a shepherd, and He began to teach them many things. And when the day was now far spent, His disciples came to Him, saying: This is a desert place, and the hour is now past." (Mark vi. 34, 35.)

REFLECTION.—Kindness of the heart of Jesus.

445. Where did this incident take place?
Near Bethsaida, on the northwestern shore of the Sea of Galilee, in an uncultivated place called a desert, where the hills are close to the sea. It was called the Plain of Butaiha, and belonged to Bethsaida.

MULTIPLICATION OF THE LOAVES AND FISHES. 159

446. How do you account for the large crowds which gathered about Jesus?

It was largely because the feast of Passover was near at hand, and the Jews, on their way to Jerusalem, went around the lake and by Perea, and hence many found themselves near where Jesus was preaching. Many fol-

lowed Jesus constantly because of His wonderful preaching and miracles.

447. What is meant by the reference to "sheep not having a shepherd"?

It means that the Scribes and Pharisees were blind to the truth, and not fit to guide the people of God. The only traditions which seemed to enter their life were all material ones, which kept them from realizing the presence of the Messias among them and the fulfilment of the prophecies in Him.

LESSON CXLIX.

TEXT.—". . . He said to Philip: Whence shall we buy bread that these may eat? And this He said to try him: for He Himself knew what He would do. Philip answered Him: Two hundred pennyworth of bread is not sufficient for them, that every one may take a little." (John vi. 5-7.)

REFLECTION.—Test of faith.

448. Why did Jesus ask Philip, since he was not the apostle who provided for their wants?

Some think it was because Philip was standing nearest to Him; while others remark that he was likely to have known most about the immediate conveniences for food, as he lived in that very neighborhood. To the apostles it must have seemed a very serious difficulty, and, as they did not fully realize the divine character of Christ, they hardly anticipated a miracle.

449. What is meant by the words "this He said to try him"?

It is thought that Jesus wished to test his faith, and to see what impression His words and miracles had made upon him. He wished to find the estimate which they had of His power, and thus see the influence of His work upon those who were His chosen followers and whose minds were not yet fully developed as to His character.

450. What is the value of the pennyworth mentioned by Philip?

A penny was a silver coin worth from fifteen to seventeen cents. It was what day-laborers received as wages. The denarius of Tiberias was the penny of the New Testament. In weight it was less than a shilling, but its purchasing power was greater. Two hundred pennies were equal to about thirty-three dollars.

LESSON CL.

Text.—"One of His disciples, Andrew, the brother of Simon Peter, saith to Him: There is a boy here that hath five barley loaves, and two fishes: but what are these among so many? Then Jesus said: Make the men sit down. Now there was much grass in the place. The men therefore sat down, in number about five thousand." (John vi. 8–10.)

Reflection.—The foresight of kindness.

451. What was the peculiar value of the barley loaves?

They were of much less value than wheat and were the ordinary coarse food of the lower orders. They probably belonged to the boy who was selling them. This would indicate a greater inability to feed the multitude with them and would enhance the miracle. They were thin cakes, baked on the side of the oven, like our large crackers.

452. What were the fishes to which Andrew referred?

They were small dried fish, ordinarily eaten with bread. A fish is found in all the symbolism of the catacombs. It represented Christ. It is found either carrying a basket of bread or lying on an altar beside bread; and thus is indicated faith in the Eucharist, which was prefigured by the multiplication of the loaves and fishes in the desert.

453. Were there none but men present at this miracle?

The Gospel mentions five thousand men, which is independent of the women and children, who were probably sitting by themselves. They sat in fifties and hundreds, as St. Mark relates, and hence could be easily counted.

LESSON CLI.

TEXT.—"And Jesus took the loaves: and when He had given thanks, He distributed to them that were sat down: in like manner also of the fishes as much as they would. And when they were filled, He said to His disciples: Gather up the fragments that remain, lest they be lost. They gathered up therefore, and filled twelve baskets." (John vi. 11–13.)

REFLECTION.—Thanksgiving for food.

454. What was the effect which they witnessed from Christ's words?

After Christ's words the crowd saw that there was food enough to supply the wants of all and a surplus enough to fill twelve baskets. This happened in a single act, in which Jesus blessed the loaves and fishes and distributed them to the multitude, all of whom saw the miracle which He performed and which was an evidence of the divine power which He claimed to possess.

455. To what was this miracle to lead?

To the promise of the Eucharist, which Christ was afterwards to institute as a sacrament, at the Last Supper. Immediately after this miracle, Christ discoursed upon the bread which He would give them, which was His flesh, for the life of the world. By those words He promised to give His flesh and blood in a new sacrament which He was to establish.

456. Where is this miracle renewed?

The miracle is renewed, every day, in the Holy Sacrament of the Altar, by which bread and wine are changed into the body and blood of Christ, and by which also in holy communion, under the appearance of bread, Jesus Christ is received daily by millions of His faithful people. We never can be sufficiently grateful to our good Saviour for His love for us, as manifested in the Eucharist.

Christ Promises the Eucharist.

Read carefully and study verses 22-72 of the Sixth Chapter of St. John's gospel.

LESSON CLII.

TEXT.—"Jesus answered, and said to them: This is the work of God, that you believe in Him whom He hath sent. They said therefore to Him: What sign therefore dost Thou shew that we may see, and may believe Thee? what dost Thou work? Our fathers did eat manna in the desert as it is written: He gave them bread from heaven to eat." (John vi. 29-31.)

REFLECTION.—Belief in Jesus Christ as one sent.

457. When did this discourse take place and where?

It took place on the Sabbath, the day after the miracle of the loaves and fishes, at Capharnaum, where the multitude found Jesus. After the miracle Jesus had retired to the mountain retreat to spend the night in prayer, and then He crossed the sea to still the tempest which threatened the apostles.

458. What is the first indication of the promise of the eucharistic bread?

It is when Jesus tells the multitude not to work for the bread which perishes, such as they had eaten the day before, but for the bread which lasts forever, which the Son of man is to give them.

459. How does Jesus answer their demand for a sign as great as the manna?

He shows that the manna did not come from Moses but from God and did not give immortality, whereas the bread He would now promise was Himself, who was to give life to the world, and who was to come from the bosom of the Father, and not fall from the skies, as the manna did.

460. How did the Jews receive this statement that Christ was the bread of life?

They murmured, at least some among them did, recalling the fact that they knew Him to be the son of Joseph, whose father and mother they knew, and they could not see how He could be the bread from heaven.

LESSON CLIII.

TEXT.—"I am the bread of life. Your fathers did eat manna in the desert, and are dead. I am the living bread, which came down from heaven. If any man eat of this bread, he shall live forever: and the bread that I will give, is My flesh for the life of the world." (John vi. 48, 49, 51, 52.)

REFLECTION.—The bread of life.

461. What does Christ mean by these words of the Gospel?

He identifies Himself with the bread which He promises

to give, and which is to maintain life. The manna did not preserve from death; but the manna was symbolical of Christ, who is the true bread.

462. What do you also notice in this passage?
Christ passes from the metaphorical bread to the real, and from the metaphorical eating to the real. Interpreters consider that with the words "I am the bread of life" Christ begins to speak of the Eucharist.

463. What do the words "My flesh" indicate?
They indicate the whole human nature of Christ, which is to be given as food and as sacrifice, and hence both sacrament and sacrifice are here foretold.

LESSON CLIV.

TEXT.—"The Jews therefore strove among themselves, saying: How can this man give us His flesh to eat? Then Jesus said to them: Amen, amen I say unto you: Except you eat the flesh of the Son of man, and drink His blood, you shall not have life in you." (John vi. 53, 54.)

REFLECTION.—The Real Presence.

464. How might the Jews have understood the words of Christ?
They might have understood them to refer to faith, as an action of the mind, or to an adoption of Christ's ideas, or His salvation, or they could take them as meaning a real eating of flesh, just as the words sounded.

465. How did they really understand them?
It is very evident from their murmuring that they understood Him to promise a real flesh to eat, otherwise there would have been no occasion for scandal, as the mere matter of faith would present no difficulty to their minds.

466. Did Christ recall them from this understanding or correct them?

He rather confirmed them in their view by asserting with an oath that unless they ate His flesh they would not have life in them. It would have been His duty in kindness to have removed false impressions, and since He did not it is evident that their appreciation of His meaning was correct.

LESSON CLV.

TEXT.—"Many therefore of His disciples hearing it, said: This saying is hard, and who can hear it? But Jesus knowing in Himself that His disciples murmured at this, said to them: Doth this scandalize you? If then you shall see the Son of man ascend up where He was before?" (John vi. 61-63.)

REFLECTION.—The mystery of divine love.

467. Can it be said that Christ meant all this in a metaphorical sense and referred to faith?

Certainly not, for in a metaphorical sense the phrase "eating of My flesh" meant reproach and insult, and this could not be intended, as Christ offers life eternal as a reward for the act. It could not mean faith, for they had faith already and Christ promised this bread as a new gift. The Jews, therefore, understood it correctly.

468. Why did He refer to His Ascension?

First, in order to correct the gross idea which they had that they were to eat His flesh as it then appeared before them. He wished to lead them to the idea that they were to eat His flesh under the appearance of bread. Secondly, He appealed to the power which would be manifested when they would see Him ascend into heaven.

469. How does this beautiful discourse close?

By the great act of faith made by Simon Peter when, after the disciples were asked if they would go away with those who were murmuring, he answered that Christ had the words of eternal life, and therefore if He promised His flesh to eat He was God and could fulfil His promise. In the Eucharist we have that fulfilment.

Parables of Christ.

Read carefully and study verses 4–15 of the Eighth Chapter of St. Luke's gospel, the Thirteenth Chapter of St. Matthew, and the Tenth to the Sixteenth Chapters of St. Luke.

LESSON CLVI.

TEXT.—"And His disciples asked Him what this parable might be. To whom He said: To you it is given to know the mystery of the kingdom of God, but to the rest in parables: that seeing they may not see, and hearing may not understand." (Luke viii. 9, 10.)

REFLECTION.—Unwillingness of people to accept the truth.

470. What is meant by a parable as found in the teachings of Christ?

A parable is an allegory under which something real in life or nature is made to point out a moral lesson. The word parable means *to place side by side,* because by the side of a truth is placed the image which represents it, and thus instruction is given.

471. Why were parables used in the instructions given by Christ?

(1) A new way of presenting the truth was needed to excite attention; (2) the people were not prepared to have the truth plainly taught; (3) it was a way by which to reach even those who did not wish to know the truth; (4) it prevented misunderstanding among the enemies of Christ who did not clearly see the full meaning.

472. Was this a common way of teaching among the Jews?

It was very common among the Jews of Palestine; but there was this difference, that while the Jews used parables to illustrate what had been said or taught, Christ used them as the foundation for His teaching.

LESSON CLVII.

TEXT.—" The sower went out to sow his seed: and as he sowed some fell by the wayside, and it was trodden down, and the fowls of the air devoured it. And other some fell upon good ground: and being sprung up, yielded fruit a hundred-fold. Now the parable is this: The seed is the word of God." (Luke viii. 5, 8, 11.)

REFLECTION.—The word of God.

473. What is the first series of parables we find in the life of Christ?

The first series of parables was given at a time when the Pharisees asserted that the words of Christ were inspired by the devil. These parables explained the work of God in the soul of man, as expressed by the practice of virtue.

474. Which were the principal parables of this epoch?

The Sower, the Cockle, the Mustard-seed, and the Leaven, all of which are told in Matt. xiii. Also the parable of the seed, told by St. Mark in fourth chapter, verses 26–29. They all relate to the kingdom of God.

475. How do we notice the development of the idea of the kingdom?

In the parable of the Sower the kingdom of God, as the seed, appears in man's soul and not in outward pomp and display. In the second the action of evil is seen in the sowing of tares by the devil. In the last two the development of the kingdom from weak beginnings to great strength is clearly shown. Like the leaven the idea of the kingdom should pervade all life.

LESSON CLVIII.

TEXT.—"And He spoke a parable also to them that were invited, marking how they chose the first seats at the table, saying to them: When thou art invited to a wedding, sit not down in the first place, lest perhaps one more honorable than thou be invited by him, and he that invited thee and him, come and say to thee: Give this man place." (Luke xiv. 7–9.)

REFLECTION.—The virtue of humility.

476. Which parables formed the second series in the public teaching of Christ?

They are thirteen in number, and included such parables as the Great Supper, the Good Samaritan, the Foolish Rich Man, the Lost Sheep, the Lost Son, and others recorded by St. Luke from the tenth to the sixteenth chapter.

477. What was the character of these parables?

They were in the nature of exhortations, and tended to show the great value of the kingdom of heaven, for which men should strive. They answered the blasphemy that Christ was working through Satan.

478. How does the value of the kingdom of heaven appear?

By the wise merchantman who, seeking for pearls, finds one of surpassing value, and sells all else in order to buy it. And so with the treasure hid in the field: the finder, knowing its value, parts with all his possessions, so as to buy the field and thus obtain the treasure. So with heaven to those who know its value.

LESSON CLIX.

TEXT.—"Therefore is the kingdom of heaven likened to a king, who would take an account of his servants. And when he had begun to take the account, one was brought to him, that owed him ten thousand talents. And the lord of that servant being moved with pity, let him go and forgave him the debt." (Matt. xviii. 23, 24, 27.)

REFLECTION.—Forgiveness of injuries.

479. What was the third series of parables?

The third series embraced those parables which Christ spoke at that moment in His life when He was persecuted and betrayed. They represented God's goodness and man's opportunities, and presented the kingdom of God in the light of reward and loss for righteous and unrighteous life.

480. How many are in this group, and what are they?

There are eight, and among them are found the parables of the Unjust Steward, the Unjust Judge, Dives and Lazarus, the Pharisee and Publican, the Wicked Servant, the Ten Virgins, and the Vineyard.

481. What made the difference of opinion among the people with reference to the parables?

It was not made by the substance or manner of these parables, but by the different standards by which the kingdom of God was judged. The Scribes and Pharisees had an entirely different standpoint from which to judge the teachings of Christ.

BIBLE TALKS.

The Bible and the People. (*Continued.*)

After the decree of Pope Benedict XIV., in 1757, no special application for permission to read the Bible in the languages of the people was necessary. All that was necessary was to see that such Bibles had the sanction of the Church, in order that the mutilated and badly translated versions might not mislead the people. On the first page of nearly every Catholic Bible you will find the letter of Pope Pius VI. written in 1778 to the archbishop of Florence in Italy, who had made a translation in Italian. Among other things he says, "At a time when a vast number of bad books, which grossly attack the Catholic religion, are circulated even among the unlearned, to the great destruction of souls, you judge exceedingly well that the faithful should be excited to the reading of the Holy Scriptures, for these are the abundant sources which ought to be left open to every one to draw from them purity of morals and of doctrine, and to eradicate the errors which are so widely spread in these times. This you have seasonably effected by publishing the sacred writings in the language of your country, suitable to every one's capacity." Those words do not sound much like a prohibition against the reading of the Bible. Notice the Pope says, "Ought to be left open to every one to draw from them purity of morals and of doctrine." Instead of hindering the people from reading the Holy Scriptures the Church urges them to read them; but she carefully guards them from the dangers of irresponsible translators or mutilated translations, that they may surely know the complete inspired word. In 1820 Pope Pius VII. wrote to the bishops of England exhorting them to encourage their people to read the Bible. Notice what the Holy Father gives as a reason for his exhortation: "Nothing can be more useful, more consolatory, and more animating; because they serve to confirm the faith, to support the hope, and to inflame the charity of the true Christian."

Our American bishops, in the last Plenary Council of Baltimore, leave no doubt as to their wishes in the matter of Bible reading. In their pastoral letter they say: "It can hardly be necessary for us to remind you, beloved brethren, that the most highly valued treasure of every family library and the most frequently and lovingly made use of should be the Holy Scriptures. We hope that no family can be found among you without a correct version of the Holy Scriptures." Every Catholic family has its Bible, and in many parishes and schools the study of the Bible is one of the regular courses. The New Testament studies are on those lines, and you are urged and encouraged to follow them, in order to thus correspond with the last grand appeal of Pope Leo XIII, for more general study of the Scriptures. And yet there are some who say, and no doubt believe, that you dare not have nor read the Bible, because your Church will not permit you. A reason often given is that Catholics refuse to take the Protestant Bible. Why should they take what they do not believe to be the Bible, because it has been mutilated, whole books have been cut out of it, and the translations have been made under the influence of a religious belief which does not admit of many of the vital truths of Christianity? This is not against the Bible, but against unauthorized translations of the Bible. Remember these facts when this argument is brought against the Church.

Miracles of Christ.

1. THE WIDOW OF NAIM.

Read carefully and study verses 11-18 of the Seventh Chapter of St. Luke's gospel.

LESSON CLX.

TEXT.—" And it came to pass afterwards, that He went into a city that is called Naim: and there went with Him His disciples and a great multitude. And when He came nigh to the gate of the city, behold a dead man was carried out, the only son of his mother, and she was a widow: and a great multitude of the city was with her." (Luke vii. 11, 12.)

REFLECTION.—Compassion of Jesus.

482. When did this event take place?

It took place in the summer of the year 28, very soon after the sermon on the mount. Christ had healed the centurion's servant and returned to Capharnaum, after which He went away, going through Galilee to Naim, and there performing the miracle.

483. Where was the city of Naim, where this miracle took place?

It was in the province of Galilee, situated about twenty-five miles from Capharnaum and seven miles from Nazareth. It is now called Nein, and is a wretched little village.

484. How did it happen that a great multitude was present?

Christ was then in the height of His popularity, and great crowds gathered to hear His wonderful preaching, following Him with great curiosity and earnestness. The opposition to Christ had not, as yet, fully developed its bitterness. There was a disposition to listen to Him, as no man had ever spoken as He did, and His miracles attested the mercy and goodness of His heart as well as His wonderful power.

LESSON CLXI.

TEXT.—"Whom when the Lord had seen, being moved with mercy towards her, He said to her: Weep not. And He came near and touched the bier. (And they that carried it, stood still.) And He said: Young man, I say to thee, arise. And he that was dead, sat up, and began to speak. And He gave him to his mother." (Luke vii. 13–15.)

REFLECTION.—Jesus the resurrection and the life.

485. Was Christ solicited to perform this miracle?

There is no record that any one asked Jesus to perform this miracle. He was moved to do it by His sympathy for the sorrowing, widowed mother. It also allowed Him to manifest His divine power and mercy, that thus He might attest His divine mission.

486. What did this miracle show to the people?

That Christ was the master of life and death, who could raise the dead to life as easily as He could perform the most ordinary actions, and hence must be God, who would one day call all men to judgment. Christ's power over death was evidenced in this miracle.

487. What effect had His words on the dead man?

Immediately he that was dead sat up and began to speak, thus evidencing that he was restored to life. The people who witnessed this were astonished and filled with fear, for they felt that one who could do such things must be a great prophet sent by God to His people. They thought His miracle was like those performed by the prophets of old, and failed fully to distinguish the divinity in Christ.

2. THE RULER'S DAUGHTER.

Read carefully and study verses 41-56 of the Eighth Chapter of St. Luke's gospel, and also verses 18-26 of the Ninth Chapter of St. Matthew.

LESSON CLXII.

TEXT.—" And behold there came a man whose name was Jairus, and he was a ruler of the synagogue: and he fell down at the feet of Jesus, beseeching Him that He would come into his house, for he had an only daughter almost twelve years old, and she was dying." (Luke viii. 41, 42.)

REFLECTION.—Test of faith.

488. Where was Christ when the call came to Him to visit the dying girl?

He was in Capharnaum in the house of Matthew, who had invited Jesus and His disciples to a feast, in order that the former friends of the tax-collector might meet Jesus and be brought under His influence.

489. Who was this ruler who besought this favor from Jesus?

He was one of the elders or presiding officers of the synagogue in Capharnaum, and was consequently a most prominent Jew. With the reverence proper to the Orientals he fell on his knees, and touched the ground with his forehead, that he might thus manifest his deep respect.

490. What was remarkable in the action of this man?

We must remark the strength of his faith, which expected from Jesus help to bring his daughter to life. It was an intelligent faith and tested by great difficulties; for he went to the house of a publican, whom the Jews despised, and asked a favor from one in whom he placed his last hope.

LESSON CLXIII.

TEXT.—"As He was yet speaking, there cometh one to the ruler of the synagogue, saying to him: Thy daughter is dead; trouble Him not. And Jesus hearing this word, answered the father of the maid: Fear not, believe only, and she shall be safe. But He taking her by the hand cried out saying: Maid, arise. And her spirit returned, and she rose immediately. . . . And her parents were astonished, whom He charged to tell no man what was done." (Luke viii. 49, 50, 54-56.)

REFLECTION.—Triumph of faith.

491. What was the difficulty which confronted the faith of Jairus?

It was that while he was asking Christ to save his daughter from death word came that she was already dead. He might have thought that if Christ had gone immediately He could have prevented death. Still, notwithstanding the bad news he seems not to have faltered.

492. What condition did Christ lay down for the extraordinary miracle?

It was that Jairus should believe in Him and all would go well with the girl. To Him nothing was impossible; but He demanded that the father recognize that the gift was to come from God, who would thus reward his belief and his confidence in Him.

493. How did the crowd regard the cheering word of Jesus?

With scorn and ridicule, for they had no faith in Him. But He disregarded their contempt, and rewarded the ruler's faith by restoring the girl to life, and thus, in the presence of an astonished crowd, He performed one of His great miracles.

The Transfiguration.

Read carefully and study verses 28-36 of the Ninth Chapter of St. Luke's gospel; also verses 1-13 of the Seventeenth Chapter of St. Matthew and verses 2-10 of the Ninth Chapter of St. Mark.

LESSON CLXIV.

TEXT.—"And it came to pass about eight days after these words, that He took Peter and James and John, and went up into a mountain to pray. And whilst He prayed, the shape of His countenance was altered: and His raiment became white and glittering." (Luke ix. 28, 29.)

REFLECTION.—The results of prayer.

494. When and where did the Transfiguration take place?

It very probably took place in the summer, about nine months before the Crucifixion. It is thought to have happened in the night, because Jesus usually prayed during the night, and the Gospel narrative speaks of His coming down from the mountain the next day, when the sleepiness of the apostles indicated an all-night vigil.

495. Can we locate the scene of the Transfiguration?

It has generally been received that it took place on Mount Thabor, and Christian art has so certified; but modern scholars are inclined to think it was not on Mount Thabor, but on Mount Hermon, in the vicinity of Cesarea Philippi.

496. What happened on the way to Cesarea?

It was then that Christ foretold His Passion—that the Son of man would be rejected and betrayed and crucified, but that He would rise again on the third day. This cast a great gloom over His disciples, and it was to dispel this gloom that Jesus determined to reveal Himself to them, or at least to the chosen ones.

497. Why did He choose but three of the twelve to witness His Transfiguration?

It may have been because they were the most advanced in knowledge of Him and were better fitted to receive the new revelation. They were His first acquaintances and the first whom He called to the apostolate. The other nine were left at the foot of the mountain.

LESSON CLXV.

TEXT.—" And behold two men were talking with Him. And they were Moses and Elias, appearing in majesty: and they spoke of His decease that He should accomplish in Jerusalem. But Peter and they that were with Him, were heavy with sleep. And awaking, they saw His glory, and the two men that stood with Him." (Luke ix. 30-32.)

REFLECTION.—The glory of God revealed.

498. What happened to Christ in the scene on the mount?

St. Matthew says: "He was transfigured before them," which means that the appearance of His countenance changed as if it were lighted up from without and within, His heavenly glory breaking forth and making His face to shine as the sun, while His garments became white as snow. (Matt. xvii. 2.)

499. Who appeared with Him and why?

Moses and Elias appeared in their glorified bodies that they might show (1) the fulfilment of the law and the prophets in Christ and bear witness to Him, and (2) that thus they might attest the complete redemption which Christ effected.

500. How did they attest the law and the prophets?

Moses was the representative of the law, for he was the law-giver of the Jews, and Christ was to transform the law into the Gospel. Moses was also a type of Christ. Elias represented the prophets, who foretold the coming of Christ and prepared the way for Him. Elias stood for those who had prophesied the Passion and glorious Resurrection of Christ.

LESSON CLXVI.

TEXT.—"And it came to pass that as they were departing from Him, Peter saith to Jesus: Master, it is good for us to be here: and let us make three tabernacles, one for Thee, and one for Moses, and one for Elias: not knowing what he said." (Luke ix. 33.)

REFLECTION.—Thanksgiving for favors.

501. Why did Jesus grant this vision to His chosen disciples?

To console them after His sad words concerning His approaching Passion. He allowed them to catch a glimpse of His dignity, that thus they might know something of the power which as king He possessed, and the Resurrection be made easy of belief.

502. What effect did it have upon the disciples?

It showed them the harmony between the Old and New Testaments, which must have appeared to them so much out of touch with one another, and thus it proved the unity of religion; and it made manifest what was in store for redeemed humanity when faithful to God.

503. What is the meaning of the words that Peter used: "not knowing what he said"?

He was so dazzled by the sight that he would have wished the heavenly messengers to remain, that the disciples might enjoy the manifestation and learn more of the dignity and majesty of the Master, whom they were now beginning to understand more fully.

LESSON CLXVII.

TEXT.—" And as he spoke these things, there came a cloud, and overshadowed them: and they were afraid, when they entered into the cloud. And a voice came out of the cloud, saying: This is My beloved Son, hear Him. And whilst the voice was uttered, Jesus was found alone. And they held their peace, and told no man in those days any of these things which they had seen." (Luke ix. 34–36.)

REFLECTION.—The testimony of God.

504. What did the bright cloud indicate?

It indicated in all probability the divine presence, which is frequently symbolized by the cloud of brightness, as on Mount Sinai to Moses, in the desert to the people, and also on the Ark between the cherubim.

505. What was the significance of the voice out of the cloud?

It was the testimony of God as to Jesus. It had been heard when John baptized Our Lord in the Jordan, and would be heard again as He approached His Passion. In proclaiming to the apostles that Jesus Christ was His Son, God also proclaimed it to the whole world.

506. Why were they warned to tell no man what they had seen?

Because the others were so worldly and so carnal in their ideas that they were not prepared to accept this heavenly testimony. It would have been misunderstood and perverted, and the human nature in Christ would not have been believed as real.

The Raising of Lazarus.

Read carefully and study verses 1-45 of the Eleventh Chapter of St. John's gospel.

LESSON CLXVIII.

TEXT.—"Now there was a certain man sick named Lazarus, of Bethania, of the town of Mary and of Martha her sister. (And Mary was she that anointed the Lord with ointment and wiped His feet with her hair: whose brother Lazarus was sick.) His sisters therefore sent to Him saying: Lord, behold, he whom Thou lovest, is sick." (John xi. 1-3.)

REFLECTION.—Sympathy in sorrow.

507. Where was Christ when He received the message of the illness of Lazarus?

He was at Bethabara, beyond the Jordan, while the home of Lazarus was in Bethany, on the Mount of Olives, about two miles south-east from Jerusalem, where he lived with his two sisters, and where Jesus made a home when He found Himself in that neighborhood. The distance between the two places was about thirty miles.

508. Is this Mary of Bethany and Mary Magdalen the one woman?

There has been much discussion about the identity of these two names; but strong opinion favors believing them to be one and the same. This also may be seen by the office for July 22d, as found in the Breviary.

509. What was the nature of the love of Jesus for them?

He loved them because they were good people who loved God, and as He visited them frequently He had also a human affection for them as a family to which He was much attached. Hence Lazarus is called His friend, because there was a special affection between them.

LESSON CLXIX.

TEXT.—" And Jesus hearing it, said to them: This sickness is not unto death, but for the glory of God, that the Son of God may be glorified by it. Now Jesus loved Martha, and her sister Mary, and Lazarus. When He had heard therefore that he was sick, He still remained in the same place two days." (John xi. 4-6.)

REFLECTION.—Duty of affection.

510. In the meantime what had happened?

Lazarus had died and was buried the same day. The sisters had sent for Jesus, and His not coming had caused all hope to disappear. They could not understand why He delayed.

511. When did Jesus arrive at Bethany?

He arrived four days after the death of Lazarus, and was

met outside the city by Martha, who, with a certain sorrowful reproach, said to Him: "Lord, if Thou hadst been here my brother had not died; but now also I know that whatsoever Thou wilt ask of God, God will give it Thee."

512. What was the answer which Jesus made to Martha's words?

He assured her that Lazarus would rise again, and that this resurrection would not be the one which would come at the last day, but here and now, as He was the resurrection and the life.

LESSON CLXX.

TEXT.—"Jesus saith: Take away the stone. . . . They took therefore the stone away: and Jesus lifting up His eyes, said: Father, I give Thee thanks that Thou hast heard Me; and I knew that Thou hearest Me always, but because of the people who stand about have I said it: that they may believe that Thou hast sent Me. When He had said these things, He cried with a loud voice: Lazarus, come forth." (John xi. 39, 41-43.)

REFLECTION.—Resurrection from sin.

513. Why did Jesus weep when told the story of Lazarus' death?

Because of the loving sympathy and tenderness of His character. He rejoices with those in joy, as at the marriage feast, and He sorrows with those in affliction. It is the love of God manifesting itself so that we may understand it.

514. What did He demand of Martha?

What He had demanded from all others who sought for His miraculous intervention, namely, a faith in God and a confidence in His power to do that which would manifest the glory of God and restore her brother to her.

515. What was the object of the prayer which Jesus uttered?

It was to teach the multitude to have recourse to God in all circumstances, and also to prove the unity of action between Him and His Father; for if the miracle be performed, then it proves His divine mission.

LESSON CLXXI.

TEXT.—"And presently he that had been dead came forth, bound feet and hands with winding-bands, and his face was bound about with a napkin. Jesus said to them: Loose him and let him go. Many therefore of the Jews who were come to Mary and Martha, and had seen the things that Jesus did, believed in Him." (John xi. 44, 45.)

REFLECTION.—New life through Christ.

516. In what did this miracle differ from that of Naim and of the daughter of Jairus?

In this, that Lazarus was several days dead, and was buried and had already entered upon corruption, so that health came to corruption as well as life to death; while as in the other cases before corruption had set in life came to the body, and the soul returned to inhabit the body it had quitted.

517. What effect had this miracle upon those who witnessed it?

Many, seeing the fact, were convinced that the power which could so operate must be divine, and that Christ was what He called Himself—the Son of God.

518. What became of Lazarus after these events?

The legends have it that he lived for thirty years afterwards, and that he and his sisters were sent to sea in a leaky boat and drifted to Marseilles, where he preached the Gospel, became bishop, established the Church and suffered martyrdom.

BIBLE TALKS.

The Bible and the People. *(Concluded.)*

We have seen that not only does our Church not forbid us to read the Bible, but that she urges us to study it carefully and religiously in order to find light and consolation. She insists on one condition, that the version used be a Catholic one, authorized by our bishops. As we have seen, this is to preserve us from the danger of being led astray by incorrect or unauthorized translations. As the Catholic acknowledges the Church as his teacher, so in his study or reading of the Bible he will seek for her interpretation of all the texts. To him the Bible is a treasury of divine knowledge, a source of the knowledge of life. In it he finds the foundations of belief and the rule of conduct for his life. We should avail ourselves of the liberty given us by the Church to open this great book and read the very words of God Himself. How much time is spent by men in reading the vain and deceitful words of men in the daily papers and in the books that flood us on every side! In the Bible God Himself speaks to us, and men value it not. See how the Jews of old read the laws of Moses, and went to them in all their trials and difficulties! See how they reverenced the Ark of the Covenant simply because it contained the tablets of stone on which God had engraven the ten commandments! How they listened to the voice of the prophets because they spoke in the name of God! How much more reverence and confidence we should have in the Book in which God has written not merely the commandments, but the history of His people, His mercy and love, as seen above all in our blessed Saviour! We read the lives of heroes and great men, warriors and statesmen; we find so much to admire in their acts and words because we think that they were great and wise. In the Bible we have characters beautiful to admire and admirable to imitate. Their deeds are the deeds of virtue and true greatness. We have Jesus Christ, our good and gentle Saviour, Our Lord and God, greater than the greatest of men, whose life is full of all that is worthy of admiration and love. He is Our Redeemer, the One who has saved us from slavery and ignorance and eternal loss. How we should love to know Him, to read His life, to learn His words! In this age, when faith is so weak and when truth is so surrounded with the dangers of error, we need to go to the word of God for light and strength. The Church bids us open this Book, as St. Augustine was bidden, that we may read what is truth and life. If we would desire to enter into the spirit of holy Church, we will study the Bible under the direction of safe spiritual guides, and thus keep God nearer to us.

How beautiful the words of Cardinal Gibbons in a sermon on the Bible: "You who are chosen soldiers of Christ should certainly have as much attachment for the Book of books as Alexander had for the Greek poet. If you rest on your pillow, armed with 'the sword of the Spirit, which is the word of God,' you will find in it the best sedative for allaying mental troubles and feverish excitement; you will repose in peace and security; for, in the language of the Psalmist, God shall overshadow thee with His shoulders and under His wings thou shalt trust. His truth shall be thy shield and buckler."

The Rich Young Man.

Read carefully and study verses 17–27 of the Tenth Chapter of St. Mark; also verses 16–30 of the Nineteenth Chapter of St. Matthew, and verses 18–30 of the Eighteenth Chapter of St. Luke.

LESSON CLXXII.

TEXT.—"And when He was gone forth into the way, a certain man running up and kneeling before Him, asked Him: Good Master, what shall I do that I may receive life everlasting? And Jesus said to him: Why callest thou Me good? None is good but one, that is God." (Mark x. 17, 18.)

REFLECTION.—Importance of salvation.

519. Where and when did this event take place?

It took place while Christ was on His way to Jerusalem, near the borders of Samaria and Galilee, just before He reached Jericho. It happened about a month before the Passion, a few weeks after the resurrection of Lazarus.

520. What had happened in the meantime?

The Jewish leaders were so excited against Christ by the raising of Lazarus, that He kept away from Jerusalem and returned to Ephrem, in the mountains of northern Judea. As He journeyed to the Jordan He healed the ten lepers, discoursed on the kingdom of God, and blessed the little children, as we may see narrated in the seventeenth and eighteenth chapters of St. Luke.

521. Who was the rich young ruler?

He was probably an elder in the synagogue, possessing great means, and was attracted to Christ by his deep religious nature. As he saw Him coming from the house where He had blessed the little children he earnestly sought an answer to his question about salvation. He, no doubt, was anxious to talk with Christ and satisfy his mind upon topics of religious life which interested him.

LESSON CLXXIII.

Text.—"Thou knowest the commandments, *Do not commit adultery, Do not kill, Do not steal, Bear not false witness, Do no fraud, Honor thy father and mother.* ... Master, all these things I have observed from my youth." (Mark x. 19, 20.)

Reflection.—Conditions of salvation.

522. What was the character of this ruler, and why did he kneel to Christ?

His character was evidently that of a young man of irreproachable life who had aspired to even higher things, yet he was filled with the idea of his own goodness, and acted, as did the Pharisees, from outward motives. He knelt to Christ because he recognized Him as a great teacher deserving of reverence. He felt that he might learn something about the spiritual life from Christ.

523. What was the object of Christ's question about Himself and goodness?

It was to find if the young man regarded Him as more than an ordinary teacher. He does not deny His own goodness as God, but He tries to find out if He be recognized as God, and thus the sincerity of the young man is put to a test which leads him to the true source of goodness, which is in God, and not in personal righteousness, which latter seemed to be the young man's idea.

524. What did Christ declare to be the conditions of eternal life?

He gave as an absolute condition of eternal life that he observe the commandments of God, which teach man's duty to God and to his fellow-man, and which must be followed in spirit as well as in letter, as Christ said, according to St. Matthew: "If thou wilt enter into life keep the commandments."

LESSON CLXXIV.

TEXT.—"And Jesus looking on him, loved him, and said to him: One thing is wanting unto thee: go, sell whatsoever thou hast, and give to the poor, and thou shalt have treasure in heaven: and come, follow Me. Who being struck sad at that saying, went away sorrowful: for he had great possessions." (Mark x. 21, 22.)

REFLECTION.—The perfect life.

525. Why did Jesus love the young man?

Because He saw that he was a noble character and was earnest in desiring to know what more was required of him beside the mere observance of the law. He saw great possibilities in him if he would only correspond to grace and make sacrifices for God, and thus perhaps become one of the chosen ministers of Christ, and aid in the work of the salvation of mankind, as well as in his own salvation, which occupied his whole attention at this particular moment, as may be seen by his question.

526. What did Christ advise him to do?

Wishing that he might lead a perfect life, He recommended that he disengage himself from his worldly possessions and give himself unreservedly to God as a disciple of Christ, whose self-denial he was called to imitate and whose ministry he was called to serve. As Christ gave him to understand, this was the surest way to attain to everlasting life.

527. How did the young man receive this condition?

The condition appeared to him to demand too much sacrifice, and he was unwilling to fulfil it. He was disappointed and grieved as he realized the difficulty of facing what seemed to be poverty, and he lacked the generous courage which might be expected from his character.

LESSON CLXXV.

TEXT.— " And Jesus looking round about, saith to His disciples : How hardly shall they, that have riches, enter into the kingdom of God ! And the disciples were astonished at His words. But Jesus again answering, saith to them : Children, how hard is it for them that trust in riches, to enter into the kingdom of God ! It is easier for a camel to pass through the eye of a needle, than for a rich man to enter into the kingdom of God." (Mark x. 23-25.)

REFLECTION.—Danger from riches.

528. What is meant by trusting in riches ?

It means attachment to them or the placing of one's dependence upon them as if they were man's only good, or his chief aim in life. This address of Christ is not intended as an attack upon the rich, so much as a warning to them. Wealth is not man's end in life; on the contrary, the inordinate love of wealth leads to his destruction, for it usurps the place of God in the hearts and minds of men who worship it.

529. What is the strength of the comparison with the camel and the needle's eye ?

Christ is thought to have used this comparison in order to express a great difficulty; for the camel was a large animal, and the eye of a needle was very small. As it was impossible for a camel to pass through the eye of a needle, so would it be for the rich to reach heaven. The needle's eye was also the name given by the Arabs to the small door found often in the city gates admitting a man but not his camel until he had unloaded all the goods attached to it. This showed the difficulty of entering heaven unless one were detached from riches. But this Arabian idea is thought not to date back to the time of Christ.

HOLY WEEK.

The Triumphal Entry into Jerusalem.

Read carefully and study verses 1-11 of the Eleventh Chapter of St. Mark's gospel; also verses 1-17 of the Twenty-first Chapter of St. Matthew; verses 29-48 of the Nineteenth Chapter of St. Luke, and verses 12-19 of the Twelfth Chapter of St. John.

LESSON CLXXVI.

TEXT.—"And when they drew nigh to Jerusalem, and were come to Bethphage, unto Mount Olivet: then Jesus sent two disciples, saying to them: Go ye into the village that is over against you, and immediately you shall find an ass tied, and a colt with her: loose them and bring them to Me: and if any man shall say anything to you, say ye, that the Lord hath need of them: and forthwith he will let them go." (Matt. xxi. 1-3.)

REFLECTION.—Christ as King.

530. What happened after the time when Christ taught the rich young ruler?

Christ went to the house of Zacheus into Jericho, and thence to Bethany, where He was visited by many Jews on the following Sabbath, after which He attended a supper in the house of Simon and was anointed by Mary. This was just before the Passion, when He was entering upon the last week of His public life.

531. Where was Jesus when He sent His disciples to the village of Bethphage?

He was on the western slope of the Mount of Olives, near Jerusalem, not far from Bethany, the home of Lazarus, and within sight of Bethphage. Here He remained to prepare for the triumphal entry into Jerusalem.

532. Who were the disciples whom Jesus sent, and what was the village?

It is thought that the two disciples were Peter and John, as may be seen in Luke xxii. 8. Bethphage, which means House of Figs, was the town to which they were sent, and this they reached by a foot-path across the gorge, in order the quicker to comply with their Master's command.

LESSON CLXXVII.

TEXT.—"Now all this was done that it might be fulfilled which was spoken by the prophet, saying: Tell ye the daughter of Sion: Behold thy King cometh to thee, meek, and sitting upon an ass and a colt the foal of her that is used to the yoke. And the disciples going did as Jesus commanded them. And they brought the ass and the colt: and laid their garments upon them, and made Him sit thereon." (Matt. xxi. 4-7.)

REFLECTION.—The fulfilment of the prophecy.

533. Who uttered the prophecy to which the Evangelist alludes?

The prophet Zacharias (ix. 9) uttered the prophecy,

which is quoted by St. Matthew. Isaias also prophesied in a similar strain. The Messias was to come to His people as a king and in the simplest manner—not as in war, but as in peace, for the ass was the symbol of peace.

534. What did this prophecy mean in its fulfilment?

It meant to show the character of the Messias, who was to offer Himself as the King whose mission was to rule the hearts of men. He came, from a sense of duty, to reveal His kingly power to the people of Jerusalem, and His kingly power foreshadowed His final triumph.

535. How did He assert His kingly power?

By claiming to be the Messias and manifesting His ability to perfectly accomplish the will of God, showing His authority over all things (1) by His message to His disciples; (2) by taking for His use what His subjects possessed. His kingship was one of love and peace.

LESSON CLXXVIII.

TEXT.—"And a very great multitude spread their garments in the way: and others cut boughs from the trees, and strewed them in the way: and the multitudes that went before, and that followed, cried, saying: Hosanna to the Son of David: blessed is He that cometh in the name of the Lord: Hosanna in the highest." (Matt. xxi. 8, 9.)

REFLECTION.—The welcome to the King.

536. What was the occasion which brought great multitudes at that time to Jerusalem?

It was the feast of Passover, which brought the Jews from all over the world to take part in the ceremonies of the feast. It is known that sometimes nearly three millions of people crowded into Jerusalem. This fact accounts for the great crowds that blocked the way of Jesus to the Temple.

537. Why did they spread their garments before Him?

This was to manifest their reverence and esteem; for it was customary to so strew the way before one whom they regarded as a king, thus to proclaim his dominion over his people and the people's obedience and reverence. Though Jesus was humble and simple, yet He was King, and Jerusalem so acknowledged it.

538. What was the meaning of the cries of the people?

They were the expressions of the joy of the people at what they had seen in the miracles which Jesus had performed. It was a mingling of praise and rejoicing, while all clamored for salvation from Him, who was God's messenger to them, for He came in the name of the Lord.

LESSON CLXXIX.

TEXT.—" And the chief priests and Scribes seeing the wonderful things that He did, and the children crying in the Temple, and saying: Hosanna to the Son of David, were moved with indignation. And leaving them, He went out of the city into Bethania: and remained there." (Matt. xxi. 15, 17.)

REFLECTION.—Abuse of grace.

539. What was the feeling of Jesus as He approached Jerusalem?

As He saw it He knew how little Jerusalem thought of God and redemption, and how ignorant she was of all God's mercies, and He wept as He remembered all that God had done for His people. He saw the destruction that was impending upon this city and people.

540. Why did Jesus enter the Temple, and what followed?

He entered it to take formal possession of His Father's house. The innocent children chanted His praise and welcomed Him, and He told the Jews that perfect praise came from the mouths of infants. He cleansed the Temple and proclaimed it His Father's house. In sorrow He went from Jerusalem and passed the night in Bethany.

The Last Supper.

Read carefully and study verses 12-26 of the Fourteenth Chapter of St. Mark's gospel; also verses 17-30 of the Twenty-sixth Chapter of St. Matthew, and verses 7-30 of the Twenty-second Chapter of St. Luke.

LESSON CLXXX.

TEXT.—" And on the first day of the Azymes the disciples came to Jesus saying: Where wilt Thou that we prepare for Thee to eat the Pasch? But Jesus said: Go ye into the city to a certain man, and say to him: The Master saith: My time is near at hand, with thee I make the Pasch with My disciples. And the disciples did as Jesus appointed to them, and they prepared the Pasch." (Matt. xxvi. 17-19.)

REFLECTION.—Love of Jesus for men.

541. Where and how did Jesus spend the time between the triumphal entry and the Last Supper?

He discoursed in the Temple and on Mount Olivet on Monday and Tuesday, giving parables, denouncing the Pharisees, and announcing His Passion. He then went to Bethany, where He spent Wednesday, and Thursday morning. In the afternoon of this latter day He sent His disciples to have the Pasch prepared.

542. What is meant by the first day of the Azymes?

The Azymes was the term used to designate the feast of the unleavened bread, because it alone was allowed. It signified the hurry with which the Jews fled from Egypt, not waiting for the bread to rise. It is also made to refer to all their afflictions while in bondage.

543. When was the Passover celebrated?

It was always celebrated at the full moon and at the beginning of the month Nisan, which was the first month of the Hebrews and corresponds to our March or April. The new moon indicated the new religious year of the Jews. In the evening after sunset, the beginning of the fifteenth day, the paschal supper was eaten.

LESSON CLXXXI.

TEXT.—"But when it was evening, He sat down with His twelve disciples. And whilst they were eating, He said: Amen I say to you, that one of you is about to betray Me. And they being very much troubled, began every one to say: Is it I, Lord? But He answering said: He that dippeth his hand with Me in the dish, he shall betray Me." (Matt. xxvi. 20–23.)

REFLECTION.—The sin of betrayal.

544. Which of the disciples were sent to prepare the Pasch?

Peter and John were selected by Christ, because they were acquainted with the city, and their duty was to furnish the room, select the lamb and have it prepared for the feast, and supply all else that might be necessary.

545. Why was the choice of place made by Christ Himself?

Because during the Passover celebration all Jerusalem was supposed to give hospitality, and all pilgrims were freely received and cared for. No doubt Christ had made previous arrangements about the place, and hence the apostles had no trouble.

546. How was the room furnished for the feast?

It was furnished with tables and couches, and prepared for the reception of guests. In this case the host was probably a disciple of Christ, but for fear of the Jews he practised his religion in secret, and hence his name is not given. He showed them to the large upper room, which was a mark of great distinction.

LESSON CLXXXII.

TEXT.—"The Son of man indeed goeth, as it is written of Him: but wo to that man, by whom the Son of man shall be betrayed: it were better for him, if that man had not been born. And Judas that betrayed Him, answering said: Is it I, Rabbi? He saith to him: Thou hast said it." (Matt. xxvi. 24, 25.)

REFLECTION.—Hypocrisy.

547. When did Jesus go to Jerusalem to the supper-room?

Late in the afternoon of Thursday, in time to comply with the law of the Passover. The twelve apostles accompanied Him and manifested some jealousy as to the places they were to occupy, and Jesus had to teach them a lesson in humility.

548. What was the first ceremony which followed?

The washing of the feet, usually done by the servants.

was done in this instance by Christ Himself, who insisted on washing the feet of His apostles who were His guests. Thus, while the law was being observed, a lesson in humility was taught them, as He, the first among them, made Himself the least.

549. What followed this act of humility?

Jesus then referred to the treachery of Judas, who had already gone to the high priests and accepted a bribe to betray Him that very night. His words might serve to call Judas to repentance or to warn the apostles of the danger which threatened them. In answer to their anxious inquiries Christ tells them that it is one of those eating bread with Him who would betray Him.

LESSON CLXXXIII.

TEXT.—"And whilst they were at supper, Jesus took bread, and blessed, and broke, and gave to His disciples, and said: Take ye, and eat: This is My body. And taking the chalice He gave thanks: and gave to them, saying: Drink ye all of this. For this is My blood of the New Testament which shall be shed for many unto remission of sins." (Matt. xxvi. 26-28.)

REFLECTION.—The Holy Eucharist.

550. What happened after the eating of the paschal lamb?

Christ then fulfilled the promise made at the multiplication of the loaves and fishes. Taking the unleavened bread and the chalice filled with wine, He blessed them and gave them to the apostles to eat and drink, saying that they were His body and His blood, thus establishing the Eucharist and giving the bread He had promised.

551. What happened at the moment these words were uttered?

These words changed the substance of bread and wine

into the substance of the body and blood of Christ. It was God who said those words, and we believe them to be true, just as He said them. This change is called the Eucharist, a Greek word meaning *thanksgiving*, because at the establishment of it He *gave thanks*, although it was at the shedding of His own blood.

552. What power did Christ then confer upon the apostles?

The power to do what He had done. For He said: " Do this for a commemoration of Me," which was accepted by them as constituting them priests of the New Law, who, in the bread and wine of the Sacrifice of the Mass, would maintain a perpetual memorial of Christ, and thus offer the Sacrifice of the New Law. This was the faith of the Apostles and of the Church which they established in the world.

Christ at Gethsemani.

Read carefully and study verses 32-42 of the Fourteenth Chapter of St. Mark; also verses 36-46 of the Twenty-sixth Chapter of St. Matthew, and verses 39-46 of the Twenty-second Chapter of St. Luke.

LESSON CLXXXIV.

TEXT.—" And they come to a farm called Gethsemani. And He saith to His disciples: Sit you here, while I pray. And He taketh Peter and James and John with Him: and He began to fear and to be heavy. And He saith to them: My soul is sorrowful even unto death: stay you here and watch." (Mark xiv. 32-34.)

REFLECTION.—Sorrow of sin.

553. What happened after the Last Supper?

Judas went out to fulfil his bargain with the high priests, and Christ discoursed at length to the other apostles about His mission. Then, having chanted the hymn prescribed by the law, they went out, crossed the brook of Cedron, and entered the Garden of Olives, where Jesus was accustomed to pray.

554. Where was the brook of Cedron?

It was a deep ravine crossed by two bridges—one on the road to St. Stephen's Gate and another leading to the Golden Gate. Cedron means *black;* and the brook was so called because its dark waters were colored by the blood of the sacrifices from the Mount of the Temple.

555. Where was the Garden of Gethsemani located?

According to St. Jerome, it lay at the foot of Mount Olivet, east of the brook of Cedron, probably not far from the present Gethsemani Garden. It was a small enclosure which in those days offered a quiet place of retreat near the olive-press. The true spot was no doubt determined during the visit of St. Helena to Jerusalem in 326, when the place of Calvary was identified.

LESSON CLXXXV.

TEXT.—"And when He was gone forward a little, He fell flat on the ground: and He prayed that if it might be, the hour might pass from Him: and He saith: Abba, Father, all things are possible to Thee, remove this chalice from Me, but not what I will, but what Thou wilt. And He cometh, and findeth them sleeping. And He saith to Peter: Simon, sleepest thou? couldst thou not watch one hour?" (Mark xiv. 35-37.)

REFLECTION.—Necessity of prayer.

556. How did He divide the apostles?
He placed eight of them as outer sentinels at the entrance to the garden, to guard against surprises and interruptions, and He bade them pray while He and the three others went into the garden. Peter, James, and John, who had witnessed His Transfiguration, were to witness His agony.

557. What was His instruction to those three apostles?
He bade them act as the inner guard, and also to watch and pray, so as to avoid temptation. Then He advanced further in, to be alone in prayer. He was some two hundred feet from them, or, as the Gospel calls it, about a stone's throw. There, kneeling, He entered into prayer and agony.

558. What was the sorrow that afflicted Christ?
It was the extreme of human sorrow. As man He was to endure this agony, which came (1) from a sense of the heinousness of sin, with which He loaded Himself; (2) from His utter abandonment and destitution of all human comfort; (3) man's ingratitude. His human nature

revolted against suffering, and in His agony He suffered all that humanity could endure.

•

LESSON CLXXXVI.

TEXT.—"Watch ye, and pray that you enter not into temptation. The spirit indeed is willing, but the flesh is weak. And going away again, He prayed, saying the same words: and when He returned He found them again asleep (for their eyes were heavy) and they knew not what to answer Him." (Mark xiv. 38-40.)

REFLECTION.—Need of watchfulness.

559. Why did Christ ask that the chalice pass away from Him?

It was so filled with suffering and trial that it seemed impossible for human nature to find strength to drink it; but the divine will in Christ asserted itself, and He accepted the chalice as God offered it. This agony showed the extent of the burden of sin which demanded such a redemption.

560. What was the answer to Christ's prayer?

Courage came to Him that He might endure the suffering. An angel came and supported Him, thus giving Him that help which His human nature demanded. Consolation and courage came as manifestations of help from God to Him.

561. What had happened to the apostles?

They were overpowered with sleep, for it was after the midnight hour, and all the excitement of the day and the forebodings for the morrow combined to weary them. St. Luke asserts that they were sleeping because of great sorrow, yet Christ reproached them for inability to watch with Him even for one hour.

LESSON CLXXXVII.

TEXT.—" And He cometh the third time, and saith to them: Sleep ye now, and take your rest. It is enough: the hour is come: behold the Son of man shall be betrayed into the hands of sinners. Rise up, let us go; behold, he that will betray Me is at hand." (Mark xiv. 41, 42.)

REFLECTION.—Ready for the sacrifice.

562. How long did the prayer and agony last?

Probably an hour, although in the gospels an hour is made to express a brief period of time. Christ went to His prayer three times; for, as we see from the Gospel, He returned to His apostles twice, only to find them drowsy and sleeping, and He went back to repeat the same prayer. He had but one thought, and that was the efficacy of His Passion.

563. What was His action then with His apostles?

He bade them take their rest if they so desired, for there would be no longer need of watching. He then stated that His hour had come and the powers of evil were about to rule, so that redemption might be effected. Rousing the three apostles, He went with them to the others, and said to them all that He was now ready for the sacrifice, as His night of prayer had fortified Him to meet the sacrifices demanded by the Passion.

564. What then followed, and with what result?

At the entrance to the garden as He returned Jesus met the band of men who, with a guard of soldiers, were coming with swords and torches to arrest Him. This was after midnight, about one o'clock Friday morning. The priests and the mob were led by the traitor apostle, Judas.

BIBLE TALKS.

It will be interesting to all the students of the New Testament studies that something be said of Douay College in France, which was one of the schools in which many of the Catholics of England received their education during the penal days. Douay is especially interesting to us in our studies, because the English translation of the New Testament most generally used and approved by the Church was made at Douay in 1609. Dr. Allen, afterwards cardinal, in 1568 founded this college, from which sprang many other English colleges in Europe. The importance of the Douay press can be best estimated by the fact that the printing of Catholic books was then prohibited in England. Bishop Challoner revised the English version and wrote several controversial works. Alban Butler's Lives of the Saints is well known, Milner's End of Controversy is in every good Catholic library, and Lingard's History of England is recognized as one of the best historical books in the language. All these men received their education at Douay. Many of the students became martyrs to the faith. We learn from the registers that in 1588 twenty-two priests and eleven laymen who had returned to England died for their religion. Douay College suffered from the French Revolution, during which the students were imprisoned, and subjected to great indignities. As a result the college was abandoned, and its last members returned to England, where they were allowed to land, owing to certain changes for the better in the laws against Catholics. The Old Testament was published at the English College at Rheims in 1582, and the New Testament at Douay in 1609, but because of the influence of Douay in the whole work it is called the Douay Bible.

Bishop Denvir, the Roman Catholic bishop of Down and Connor, in Ireland, published, in 1853, an official approbation of a new edition of the Douay Bible. Several editions of the Douay Bible have been published in the United States. In 1871 a new edition was prepared, under the direction of Dr. John Gilmary Shea. The text of Bishop Challoner's own edition of 1750 was followed, typographical errors were corrected, and the punctuation and the orthography of proper names were made to conform with the standard edition of the Vulgate of 1592.

THE DAY OF THE PASSION.

The Betrayal.

Read carefully and study verses 2–12 of the Eighteenth Chapter of St. John; verses 47–54 of the Twenty-second Chapter of St. Luke; verses 43–52 of the Fourteenth Chapter of St. Mark; and verses 47–56 of the Twenty-sixth Chapter of St. Matthew.

LESSON CLXXXVIII.

TEXT.—"And Judas also, who betrayed Him, knew the place: because Jesus had often resorted thither together with His disciples. Judas therefore having received a band of soldiers, and servants from the chief priests and the Pharisees, cometh thither with lanterns and torches and weapons." (John xviii. 2, 3.)

REFLECTION.—Wickedness of heart.

565. While Jesus was at prayer in Gethsemani what was happening in Jerusalem?

Judas was conspiring with the chief priests, for after the Last Supper he went to the palace of the high priest, probably to that of Annas, who seemed to direct affairs. Here he made known the way by which Christ might be taken, and had orders issued as to the course to pursue.

566. What was the agreement as to signals between Judas and the soldiers?

That he would recognize Christ and make Him known to them by the kiss with which he would greet Him. The kiss was the usual sign of salutation among the ancients. At this signal they were to seize Him and bear Him away to the high priest, who would immediately move for his punishment.

567. Why did the high priest seek the power of the Roman government?

Because the Jews had no power to inflict capital punishment, and consequently the Sanhedrim had neither soldiers nor regularly armed men at its disposal. The Romans would not tolerate such among the Jews in Jerusalem. The Temple guard were mere police and were neither armed nor trained. For this reason Roman soldiers accompanied the band which sought Jesus.

LESSON CLXXXIX.

TEXT.—"Jesus therefore knowing all things that should come upon Him, went forth, and said to them: Whom seek ye? They answered Him: Jesus of Nazareth. Jesus saith to them: I am He. And Judas also, who betrayed Him, stood with them. As soon therefore as He had said to them: I am He: they went backward, and fell to the ground." (John xviii. 4-6.)

REFLECTION.—The meekness of the Saviour.

568. Why did they carry clubs and lanterns?

The Jews were afraid of the apostles and the people, and

thought Jesus might be hiding in the ravine or in some dark spot in the garden. The attack was made after the midnight hour lest the multitude, thinking well of all that Jesus had done, might go to His aid and frustrate their plans.

569. What was the action of Judas?

He went in advance of the band and reached Jesus just as He had roused His apostles from sleep, and saluted Him with the words, "Hail, Rabbi," or Master, kissed Him, and thus made Him known to the soldiers.

570. What was the manner of the reception Judas received from Jesus?

Jesus did not turn from the traitor, but returned the kiss, saying, with His usual civility, but in a tone of stern reproach: "Friend, why art thou come?" and then as if answering his gesture, He added: "Judas, dost thou betray the Son of man with a kiss?"

LESSON CXC.

TEXT.—"Again therefore He asked them: Whom seek ye? And they said: Jesus of Nazareth. Jesus answered: I have told you, that I am He: if therefore you seek Me, let these go their way. That the word might be fulfilled which He said: Of them whom Thou hast given Me, I have not lost any one." (John xviii. 7–9.)

REFLECTION.—Sense of responsibility.

571. What did Jesus do after His reproach to Judas?

He left the traitor and advanced to the mob and asked them whom they sought, and when they answered that they sought Jesus of Nazareth, He boldly told them He was the man, and presented Himself to them to be taken.

572. What effect had these words on them?

They seemed to be dazed, for they had expected resistance or cowardly fear; but the nobility of the man filled them with awe. As if conscience-stricken, they seemed unable to act, and under the influence of the calm majesty of Christ they fell to the ground.

573. What followed this acknowledgment of Christ's power?

Christ again asked them whom they sought, and His words aroused the leaders to a sense of what they came to do. They immediately laid hands on Him and binding Him prepared to take Him away to judgment.

LESSON CXCI.

TEXT.—"Then Simon Peter having a sword, drew it: and struck the servant of the high priest: and cut off his right ear. And the name of the servant was Malchus. Jesus therefore said to Peter: Put up thy sword into the scabbard. The chalice which My Father hath given Me, shall I not drink it? Then the band, and the tribune, and the servants of the Jews took Jesus, and bound Him." (John xviii. 10-12.)

REFLECTION.—Imprudent zeal.

574. What was the thoughtful care which Christ exercised?

He desired to protect His disciples from the crowd and asked that they be let go, that thus they might meet no danger at the hands of the mob, whose only thought was the arrest and punishment of their Master.

575. What was the action of Peter when he saw the outrage committed?

He drew his sword and struck at Malchus, the servant of the high priest, who probably led the band; but Christ needed no material aid, as He could, if He wished, have had legions of angels to protect Him against the whole army of

Rome. He healed the ear of Malchus, and thus saved Peter from violence.

576. What happened after this evidence of zeal on the part of Peter?
Jesus was bound as if He were a robber, and they carried Him away as a malefactor; while the apostles, with the exception of one, not daring to stand near Him, fled for safety lest they should be punished for resisting authority.

Christ before the High Priest.

Read carefully and study verses 53-64 of the Fourteenth Chapter of St. Mark; verses 47-75 of the Twenty-sixth Chapter of St. Matthew; verses 47-65 of the Twenty-second Chapter of St. Luke; and verses 2-27 of the Eighteenth Chapter of St. John.

LESSON CXCII.

TEXT.—"And they brought Jesus to the high priest: and all the priests and the Scribes and the ancients assembled together. And Peter followed Him afar off even into the court of the high priest: and he sat with the servants at the fire, and warmed himself. And the chief priests and all the council sought for evidence against Jesus, that they might put Him to death, and found none." (Mark xiv. 53-55.)

REFLECTION.— False accusation.

577. Who was the high priest who exercised authority at that time?

Annas was regarded as the legitimate high priest, but he had been deposed by the Romans, and his son-in-law, Caiphas, appointed by the Romans, was acting in his place. In the minds of the Jews there seemed to be some doubt as to Caiphas' authority, and hence Jesus was brought before Annas in the palace of Caiphas. This happened between one and two o'clock Friday morning.

578. What happened after this preliminary examination by Annas?

Jesus was then brought before Caiphas, who while waiting for the Sanhedrim or council to assemble asked many questions about the teaching and discipline of Christ. The answer of Christ was that everybody knew His teaching and it was easy to learn it from the people who had heard it. This brought a blow from an officer who stood near.

579. What was the character of the Sanhedrim which should try such cases?

The Sanhedrim was composed of seventy members selected (1) from the chief priests, who were at the head of the twenty-four priestly classes, (2) from the Scribes, learned in the law, and (3) from the elders or rulers, who were of great influence with the people. It was against the customs of the Jews to hold a meeting at night for capital offences, and it was a flagrant violation of all traditions to hold it at Passover.

LESSON CXCIII.

TEXT.—" For many bore false witness against Him: and their evidences were not agreeing. And some rising up, bore false witness against Him, saying: We heard Him say: I will destroy this Temple made with hands, and within three days I will build another not made with hands. And their witness did not agree." (Mark xiv. 56-59.)

REFLECTION.—Sin of perjury.

580. How did the court desire to make out the case?

It was not with a desire for the truth, but it was to condemn Christ. They secured the prisoner and then set out to condemn Him without regard to anything but their hatred and prejudice. They determined to put Him to death, and sought for evidence to justify their decision.

581. What difficulties lay in their way?

The spotless life of Christ, His goodness, and the correctness of His teaching made it impossible to find witnesses who could truthfully testify against Him. According to the law it was necessary to have at least two witnesses.

582. What then did they resort to in order to condemn Him?

They suborned many witnesses, but their testimony did not agree. At last they found two men who swore that He said things against the Temple, and as this was a capital offence because of the veneration for the Temple, it was judged sufficient.

LESSON CXCIV.

TEXT.—"And the high priest rising up in the midst, asked Jesus, saying: Answerest Thou nothing to the things that are laid to Thy charge by these men? But He held His peace, and answered nothing. Again the high priest asked Him, and said to Him: Art Thou the Christ the Son of the blessed God? And Jesus said to him: I am, and you shall see the Son of man sitting on the right hand of the power of God, and coming with the clouds of heaven." (Mark xiv. 60-62.)

REFLECTION.—Unjust condemnation.

583. What did the high priest do when this testimony was adduced?

He advanced to the open place where Jesus stood before the council, and strove to force Him to speak and criminate Himself; but Jesus was silent, as the contradictory evidence of the witnesses was sufficient refutation of the charges brought against Him. Even to the high priest's question Jesus answered nothing.

584. What then did the high priest do?

Failing to get an answer to the statements of the witnesses, he questioned Christ directly as to His character, hoping that thus he might find cause for judgment. Putting it as a matter of oath, he asked if He were the Christ, the Son of the blessed God. If He confessed He would be condemned for blasphemy; if He denied He would be proved an impostor, as He had claimed to be the Christ.

585. How did Christ meet this question?

As He had a mission to men, He found it necessary to answer it directly—for if He refused to speak it would be taken as a denial. He answered candidly that He was the Christ, and added that they would see the Son of man sitting on the right hand of the power of God and coming with the clouds of heaven.

LESSON CXCV.

TEXT.—"Then the high priest rending his garments, saith: What need we any farther witnesses? You have heard the blasphemy: what think you? Who all condemned Him to be guilty of death. And some began to spit on Him, and to cover His face, and to buffet Him and to say unto Him: Prophesy: and the servants struck Him with the palms of their hands." (Mark xiv. 63-65.)

REFLECTION.—Wickedness of the high priest.

586. What was the high priest's action at these words of Christ?

He tore his garments in a most tragic manner to express his horror at what he wanted the council to regard as a great blasphemy, although but one witness had asserted that he had heard Christ say that He would "destroy the Temple and build it up again." No attempt was made to interpret its meaning, but in malicious misunderstanding judgment was called for.

587. How did the council act?

It condemned Christ to death for what it falsely called His blasphemy. No examination was made, and thus it is apparent that none but the enemies of Christ were present at the meeting.

588. Did the Sanhedrim pass sentence at that time?

No, it did not act immediately, as it was night, and the Roman law would not allow the sentence of death to be pronounced until dawn. Though the council settled the question, the members adjourned until morning, when they could legally condemn Jesus to death.

Jesus before Pilate.

Read carefully and study verses 1–12 of the Twenty-third Chapter of St. Luke; verses 1–26 of the Twenty-seventh Chapter of St. Matthew; verses 1–5 of the Fifteenth Chapter of St. Mark; verses 28–38 of the Eighteenth Chapter of St. John.

LESSON CXCVI.

TEXT.—"And when morning was come, all the chief priests and ancients of the people took counsel against Jesus, that they might put Him to death. And they brought Him bound, and delivered Him to Pontius Pilate the governor." (Matt. xxvii. 1, 2.)

REFLECTION.—Obedience to conscience.

589. Why was Jesus sent to Pilate?

Because Pilate was the Roman governor, and he alone, as

such, had power to condemn to death. A short time before Christ's public life began the Sanhedrim had lost this power, and hence it became necessary not merely to prove violation of the Jewish law, but also treason against Cæsar.

590. Where did this hearing take place?
In the judgment hall of Pilate, which was probably in the tower of Antonia in Jerusalem, outside the northwest corner of the Temple area. It was held about half-past five Friday morning and after the Sanhedrim had judged Christ worthy of death. Christ had been bound again as a malefactor, and tradition has it that there was also a cord around His neck.

591. Who was this Pontius Pilate?
He belonged to an ancient knightly family of Rome, and came to Judea about the year 26, and was in office ten years. The capital was in Cesarea, but during the feasts he was in Jerusalem to keep order. He hated the Jews, and lost no opportunity of showing it in his judgments. But he had the old Roman respect for law, and as a judge acted sternly but, as he thought, justly.

LESSON CXCVII.

TEXT.—"And Jesus stood before the governor, and the governor asked Him, saying: Art Thou the King of the Jews? Jesus saith to him: Thou sayest it. And when He was accused by the chief priests and ancients, He answered nothing. Then Pilate saith to Him: Dost not Thou hear how great testimonies they allege against Thee? And He answered him to never a word, so that the governor wondered exceedingly." (Matt. xxvii. 11-14.)

REFLECTION.—Hypocrisy of the Pharisees.

592. Where was the first accusation made?
It was made outside the judgment hall, and Pilate went out to hear it. The Jews refused to enter within the hall,

because their traditions made entrance to a Gentile house during the feast of Passover an impurity. They scrupled the violation of a tradition, but hesitated not to make false accusations against a good man.

593. What was their accusation to Pilate?

They accused Christ (1) of sedition in perverting the nation; (2) of refusing to pay tribute to Cæsar; (3) of making Himself a king. They said nothing of blasphemy, for which the Sanhedrim condemned him, because this would have no influence with the Roman governor.

594. What followed these accusations?

Pilate questioned Christ privately as he entered the hall where Christ was with the guards, for he had not heard the accusations. Pilate ignored the first two accusations and questioned about the third, asking Christ if He was the King of the Jews; and Christ answered, strongly and firmly, "Thou sayest it."

LESSON CXCVIII.

TEXT.—" And Pilate said to the chief priests and to the multitudes: I find no cause in this man. But they were more earnest, saying: He stirreth up the people, teaching throughout all Judea, beginning from Galilee to this place. But Pilate hearing Galilee, asked if the man were of Galilee. And when he understood that He was of Herod's jurisdiction, he sent Him away to Herod, who was also himself at Jerusalem in those days." (Luke xxiii. 4–7.)

REFLECTION.—Weakness of Pilate.

595. What was Pilate's judgment?

He went out of the hall to the spot where the Jewish leaders were, and declared to them that he found no grounds for a sentence of death in the accusation against Christ. But when he heard the angry Jews mention Galilee he thought of Herod, who had jurisdiction in Galilee, and, although he found Christ guiltless, yet he sent Him as a malefactor to Herod, whom he despised with all the other Galileans. He hoped thus to secure the acquittal of Christ.

596. How did Herod receive Christ?

With great joy, for he hoped to induce Him to perform some miracles, for he had heard such wonderful things about Him. This was Herod Antipas, tetrarch of Galilee, the adulterer who had murdered John the Baptist. He was a Jew by religion, and was in Jerusalem attending the Passover. His capital was in Tiberias, on the Sea of Galilee.

597. How did Jesus answer his many demands?

By absolute silence even in the presence of the violent accusations of the chief priests, who used every means to prejudice Herod against Him. This silence irritated Herod so that he mocked and ridiculed Him, sending Him clothed as a king to Pilate.

LESSON CXCIX.

TEXT.—" And Herod seeing Jesus, was very glad; for he was desirous of a long time to see Him, because he had heard many things of Him, and he hoped to see some sign wrought by Him. And He questioned Him in many words. But He answered him nothing. And the chief priests and the Scribes stood by earnestly accusing Him. And Herod with his army set Him at naught; and mocked Him, putting on Him a white garment, and sent Him back to Pilate. And Herod and Pilate were made friends that same day: for before they were enemies one to another." (Luke xxiii. 8-12.)

REFLECTION.—Herod's deceit.

598. What was the result of Pilate's action?

Herod and he, who had been at enmity for many years, were made friends by this act. They had quarrelled over the matter of jurisdiction, and the sending back and forth of so important a prisoner settled all their differences.

599. Why was Christ silent in the presence of Herod?

Because He despised the man on account of his wicked life. Pilate was a pagan, but Herod was a Jew who lived in public sin, and because of it had murdered the great prophet, John the Baptist. He also knew it was useless to say or do anything on this occasion, for Herod was opposed to Him and His teaching, and to perform a miracle would be to gratify an idle and morbid curiosity.

600. What is to be remarked in these trials?

The absolute injustice towards the accused, whose case was not tried at all, as it seemed to be taken for granted that He was guilty anyway, and nothing that He could say would benefit Him. The calm dignity of Christ is in marked contrast with the hatred of His accusers and the unfairness of His judges.

Jesus Condemned to Death.

Read carefully and study verses 13-25 of the Twenty-third Chapter of St. Luke; verses 15-30 of the Twenty-seventh Chapter of St. Matthew; verses 6-19 of the Fifteenth Chapter of St. Mark; verses 39, 40 of the Eighteenth and verses 1-16 of the Nineteenth Chapter of St. John.

LESSON CC.

TEXT.—" And Pilate calling together the chief priests, and the magistrates, and the people, said to them: You have presented unto me this man, as one that perverteth the people, and behold I having examined Him before you, find no cause in this man in those things wherein you accuse Him. No, nor Herod neither: for I sent you to him, and behold, nothing worthy of death is done to Him. I will chastise Him therefore and release Him." (Luke xxiii. 13-16.)

REFLECTION.—Wicked judgment.

601. What was Pilate's feeling towards Jesus?

He felt that He was unjustly accused and he made

another effort to release Him; yet he was afraid to acquit Him without consulting with the leaders of the Sanhedrim who had declared Him worthy of death. He feared their opposition, and yet he wished to avoid condemning an innocent man.

602. What did Pilate do to save Jesus?

He went out of the hall to talk with the Jews who still remained outside, and for the first time he consulted with the people as well as the priests, for he thought that perhaps the people would defend Christ, or demand His release in view of what Christ had done for them by His teachings and His miracles.

603. What was Pilate's answer to the charges made against Jesus?

He told the priests and people that he had carefully examined the accusation of sedition, and that neither he nor Herod had been able to find any proof of the charge, and consequently, as an innocent man, He should be dismissed from custody.

LESSON CCI.

TEXT.—"Now of necessity he was to release unto them one upon the feast-day. But the whole multitude together cried out, saying: Away with this man, and release unto us Barabbas, who for a certain sedition made in the city and for a murder, was cast into prison." (Luke xxiii. 17-19.)

REFLECTION.—Choice of Barabbas.

604. What was the compromise which Pilate offered?

That Jesus should be scourged and sent away. Scourging was a part of the punishment of crucifixion, but Pilate suggested it not as a part, but as a substitute, which he thought might placate the Jews and thus save Jesus from death. Scourging among the Romans was very severe, the whips being armed with bones or lead, so as to tear the flesh.

605. What should Pilate have done?

He should have done what justice demanded, and that was that an innocent man be set free. He was impressed by the mildness of Christ, and besides his wife had counselled him to have nothing to do with Him, as she had been troubled about it in her dreams. But his past actions had incensed the Jews against him, and he feared to further provoke them.

606. What was the custom of release to which he referred?

It was the custom for the Roman governor at the feast of the Passover to pardon one criminal condemned to death, and thus placate the populace, and show some recognition of the great feast which commemorated the deliverance of the Jews from the bondage of Egypt.

LESSON CCII.

TEXT.—"And Pilate again spoke to them, desiring to release Jesus. But they cried again, saying: Crucify Him, crucify Him. And he said to them the third time: Why, what evil hath this man done? I find no cause of death in Him: I will chastise Him therefore, and let Him go." (Luke xxiii. 20-22.)

REFLECTION.—Pilate's failure to do justice.

607. Who was this Barabbas, and why was he chosen?

He was a prominent figure in the outbreaks against Roman cruelty, and led an insurrection in which murder and robbery were committed. It was instigated by Pilate's action in taking sacred money for the construction of aqueducts. Revolt against this action made Barabbas a favorite with the populace, who preferred him to Christ.

608. How did Pilate regard this choice?

He was astonished, as he felt confident that Christ would be chosen in preference to a vile murderer, and again he asserted the innocence of Christ, demanding that they show what evil He had done. But the cries of the chief priests excited the mob, hence the multitude would have no one released but Barabbas.

609. What did Pilate do before the final decision?

He took water and washed his hands before the people, that he might thus proclaim that his hands were innocent of the blood of Christ, as if any act of his could free him from the guilt of condemning a man whom he declared innocent. He could not put it upon the Jews, no matter how willing they were to accept it.

LESSON CCIII.

TEXT.—"And Pilate gave sentence that it should be as they required. And he released unto them him who for murder and sedition had been cast into prison, whom they had desired, but Jesus he delivered up to their will." (Luke xxiii. 24, 25.)

REFLECTION.—The denial of God.

610. Where and when did Pilate declare sentence?

After ascending what was known as the judgment-seat, outside the pretorium, in the place called the Pavement, yielding to the demands of the mob, Pilate solemnly delivered the final decree, passing Christ over to His executioners. This took place between six and seven o'clock, Friday morning.

611. What happened after the sentence?

After Pilate had given the sentence, Christ was handed over to the soldiers, who heaped insults upon Him, placing upon His head a crown of thorns which was exceedingly painful, as it was woven of a plant with small sharp spines. He was then clothed with a purple robe, in mockery of His claim to be considered a king, and was reviled and taunted by the soldiers, who beat and bruised Him, subjecting Him to all sorts of indignities.

612. What was Pilate's last act?

Thinking that the sight of this innocent man suffering and bleeding might satisfy their hate, Pilate presented Christ to the populace, saying: "Behold your King." But they cried: "We have no king but Cæsar," thus attesting their loyalty to the empire and showing the fulfilment of the prophecy that the kingly power had departed from Judea. Christ was then handed over to the soldiers for crucifixion.

The Crucifixion.

Read carefully and study verses 20–47 of the Fifteenth Chapter of St. Mark; verses 31–66 of the Twenty-seventh Chapter of St. Matthew; verses 25–56 of the Twenty-third Chapter of St. Luke; verses 16–42 of the Nineteenth Chapter of St. John.

LESSON CCIV.

TEXT.—"And as they led Him away, they laid hold of one Simon of Cyrene coming from the country: and they laid the cross on him to carry after Jesus. And there followed Him a great multitude of people, and of women: who bewailed and lamented Him. But Jesus turning to them, said: Daughters of Jerusalem, weep not over Me, but weep for yourselves, and for your children." (Luke xxiii. 26–28.)

REFLECTION.—Weep for sin.

613. What was the nature of the procession as it left Pilate's house?

In advance was a soldier bearing a white wooden board

marking the character of the crime alleged. Then came four soldiers in charge of a centurion guarding Jesus as He bore the cross on His shoulders. After Him came the two robbers who were ordered to be crucified with Him, and each had a guard of four soldiers. All that was necessary for the crucifixion was brought by the soldiers.

614. Who were the women whom Jesus met on the way?

They were good, pious women of Jerusalem who, attracted by the crowd, followed in the throng, and were afflicted by the sight of the good man suffering. Perhaps among them were some whose children had been blessed by Him. He bade them weep for sin and for those who were crucifying Him.

615. Who was Simon, and why was he called upon to help in the crucifixion?

He was from Cyrene, a Jew of northern Africa, and was forced by the soldiers to help Christ when He fell under the weight of His heavy cross. He afterwards became a Christian and preached the Gospel in Spain, and, with his two sons, Rufus and Alexander, did much for the Church of the Saviour whose cross he bore, although at the time he felt this enforced action a disgrace.

LESSON CCV.

TEXT.—" And there were also two other malefactors led with Him to be put to death. And when they were come to the place which is called Calvary, they crucified Him there: and the robbers, one on the right hand, and the other on the left." (Luke xxiii. 32, 33.)

REFLECTION.—Ignominy of the cross.

616. Where was Calvary, and what did its name signify?

Calvary was a knoll outside the north wall of the city

about one hundred yards distant, on a thoroughfare leading to the country. It was known as the Place of the Skull, because of its peculiar round top. It was known to the Jews as Golgotha, or Hill of Death, and this in Latin was *Calvaria.*

617. When they arrived there what happened?
Jesus was stripped of His clothes, His arms stretched upon the cross-beam and His hands nailed to the wood. His feet were pierced with nails, and the cross with its bleeding Victim raised from the ground and planted in the hole made for it.

618. What was given to Jesus to soothe His suffering?
They gave Him a draught of strong wine mixed with a powerful narcotic of myrrh, so as to stupefy Him and deaden all consciousness. But Jesus simply tasted it and then refused to drink, as He wished that the sacrifice should be complete even in the suffering which He endured.

LESSON CCVI.

TEXT.—"And the people stood beholding, and the rulers with them derided Him, saying: He saved others, let Him save Himself, if He be Christ, the elect of God. And the soldiers also mocked Him, coming to Him, and offering Him vinegar, and saying: If Thou be the King of the Jews, save Thyself." (Luke xxiii. 35-37.)

REFLECTION.—Mockery of Christ.

619. What was done with the two thieves?
They were also stripped and crucified, and their crosses raised on either side of that of Christ; and thus was fulfilled the prophecy found in Isaias liii. 12 that He was reputed among the wicked. Dismas is said to have been

the name of the one on His right, and Gesmas the one on His left.

620. What were the Jews doing while Jesus hung on the cross?

They were casting lots for His garments. His outer garment, the girdle, and the sandals were not so valuable, but the seamless woven inner garment was the one that they played for, while they mocked and ridiculed Him with most terrible blasphemy.

621. What was the burden of the utterances of Jesus on the cross?

He prayed to His Father to forgive His executioners because of their ignorance. He confided the care of His mother to St. John, pardoned the penitent thief, gave expression to the agony He suffered in His thirst and abandonment, and commended His soul to His Father.

LESSON CCVII.

TEXT.—"And one of those robbers who were hanged, blasphemed Him, saying: If Thou be Christ, save Thyself, and us. But the other answering, rebuked him, saying: Neither dost thou fear God, seeing thou art under the same condemnation? And he said to Jesus: Lord, remember me when Thou shalt come into Thy kingdom. And Jesus said to him: Amen I say to thee, this day thou shalt be with Me in paradise. And Jesus crying with a loud voice, said: Father, into Thy hands I commend My spirit. And saying this, He gave up the ghost." (Luke xxiii. 39, 40, 42, 43, 46.)

REFLECTION.—The pardon to repentance.

622. What was the effect on creation?

A darkness came over the land for three hours, as if to show the success of the powers of darkness over Christ and to express the revulsion of nature against man's ingratitude to God, and his blasphemous act against the Redeemer.

The veil of the Temple hanging between the holy place and the Holy of holies was rent in two, thus showing that the way to the holy place was now open for all men.

623. What effect had all this on the bystanders?

It produced a great impression upon all, and especially upon the centurion, or the officer who had charge of the soldiers. He exclaimed that this was indeed the Son of God, and he became a Christian, while many fled at witnessing the exhibition of nature in the darkness and the earthquake. Quite a number confessed their belief in Him.

624. What was the last act in this divine tragedy?

Accepting the will of His heavenly Father, Jesus felt the sweet influence of the paternal love. He resigned His soul into His Father's hands; exclaiming that all was consummated He gave up His spirit and the redemption was accomplished.

THE DAYS OF TRIUMPH.

The Resurrection.

Read carefully and study verses 1-12 of the Twenty-fourth Chapter of St. Luke; verses 1-15 of the Twenty-eighth Chapter of St. Matthew; verses 1-11 of the Sixteenth Chapter of St. Mark; verses 1-16 of the Twentieth Chapter of St. John.

LESSON CCVIII.

TEXT.—"And on the first day of the week very early in the morning they came to the sepulchre, bringing the spices which they had prepared: and they found the stone rolled back from the sepulchre. And going in, they found not the body of the Lord Jesus." (Luke xxiv. 1-3.)

REFLECTION.—The power of Christ.

625. What did the soldiers do to the body of the dead Christ?

One of them pierced His side with a lance and from it

came blood and water. This wound was to give to St. Thomas the visible proof that Christ was really risen from the dead. It was customary to break the bones of the crucified, but as Christ was dead the soldiers omitted this, and satisfied themselves with the piercing of the side.

626. What did the disciples do?

They got permission from Pilate to take the body from the cross and place it in the sepulchre which belonged to Joseph of Arimathea, a wealthy and prominent member of the Sanhedrim. But the Jews insisted that the sepulchre be sealed up, and a guard placed about it so as to prevent deception in the fulfilment of the Resurrection promise.

627. What had Christ foretold?

He had constantly and publicly said that on the third day He would rise again, and that His Resurrection was to be the proof of His divinity, and the establishment of the truth of His mission. That the Jews so understood it is evident from the demands for a seal and a guard.

LESSON CCIX.

TEXT.—"And it came to pass, as they were astonished in their mind at this, behold two men stood by them in shining apparel. And as they were afraid and bowed down their countenance towards the ground, they said unto them: Why seek you the living with the dead? He is not here, but is risen: remember how He spoke unto you, when He was yet in Galilee." (Luke xxiv. 4-6.)

REFLECTION.—The risen Saviour.

628. How long was Christ in the tomb?

He was three days in the tomb, or at least a part of three days: Friday afternoon, the whole of Saturday, and part of Sunday, which began at sunset Saturday evening. The Jews counted the parts of a day as a whole day. All Jerusalem was anxious, and especially the disciples and those who believed in Christ, as well as the high priests, for they remembered the prophecy of the Resurrection.

629. What happened on Easter morning?

Something like an earthquake shook the earth, and an angel of bright countenance rolled away the great stone, and thus exposed to view the empty sepulchre. Christ was risen, as He had said, and went to Galilee, and thus the prophecies were fulfilled, and Christ's divine nature was manifested to men.

630. What became of the guards?

They were frightened at the sight and fled in terror to Jerusalem to tell the high priests and the Roman officials what had happened. The chief priests, to continue their fraud, bade them say that while they slept the disciples of Jesus came and took His body away. This made them poor witnesses of what they confessed not to have seen.

The Women of the Resurrection.

Read carefully and study verses 7-12 of the Twenty-fourth Chapter of St. Luke; verses 1-11 of the Sixteenth Chapter of St. Mark; and verses 11-18 of the Twentieth Chapter of St. John.

LESSON CCX.

TEXT.—" Saying : The Son of man must be delivered into the hands of sinful men, and be crucified, and the third day rise again. And they remembered His words. And going back from the sepulchre, they told all these things to the eleven, and to all the rest." (Luke xxiv. 7-9.)

REFLECTION.—Joy of the Resurrection.

631. How did the information about the Resurrection reach the disciples?

The holy women, who were watching for the morning, went with fear and trembling to the sepulchre, that they might anoint the body of Jesus, according to the custom which prevailed among the Jews; but they were afraid that the stone at the door of the tomb could not be removed. They were astonished when they saw the sepulchre open, and a young man in white seated therein. To their anxious inquiries he answered by reminding them of Christ's promise, and told them of its fulfilment.

632. What did the holy women then do?

Mary Magdalen told Peter and John and the other apostles what they saw, but the story was received as an idle tale, or a woman's vision. This assures us that the apostles could not easily be deluded or deceived. They demanded substantial proof of Christ's Resurrection before they would believe it. They did not at that time fully under-

stand Christ or the prophecies concerning Him, and hence were slow to believe what they did not see.

633. What did they do to satisfy themselves?

As soon as they heard the story of the Resurrection from the holy women, Peter and John went in great haste to the tomb and investigated for themselves, and when they satisfied themselves as to the truth of the story they returned to assure the rest of the apostles that Christ was truly risen. They had examined the place, and were certain that Christ had risen as He had promised. They realized that later on they would more fully understand what had happened.

LESSON CCXI.

TEXT.—"And it was Mary Magdalen, and Joanna, and Mary of James, and the other women that were with them, who told these things to the apostles. And these words seemed to them as idle tales: and they did not believe them. But Peter rising up ran to the sepulchre: and stooping down he saw the linen cloths laid by themselves, and went away wondering in himself at that which was come to pass." (Luke xxiv. 10-12.)

REFLECTION.—The truth of Christ.

634. How often did Christ appear to His disciples and followers?

At least eleven times: first to Mary Magdalen, then to the holy women, then to Peter, and afterwards several times to the apostles and the people, thus assuring them that He was truly risen from the dead and was the true Messias as claimed. They were all ready to die for this belief in the Resurrection.

635. Where do you find a good proof of the Resurrection?

One proof may be found in the belief of the apostles, who had nothing to gain by deceit, especially when they had to die for their belief. Were Jesus not risen, then they were called to maintain the religion of an impostor. That weak, cowardly men would lend themselves to an imposture is not to be believed when you consider that eleven of them preached the Resurrection and died in vindication of it.

636. What may be offered as another proof?

Another proof may be found in the fact that the pagan world became Christian and the religion of Christ became the doctrine of the world, in spite of the fact that it appealed to self-denial and not to indulgence, and also that it antagonized the world's maxims and man's inclinations. What pagan philosophy could not do in converting the world to its theories Christian faith did, as we see from history.

The Risen Christ with His Apostles.

Read carefully and study verses 13-53 of the Twenty-fourth Chapter of St. Luke; verses 19-31 of the Twentieth Chapter and verses 1-25 of the Twenty-first Chapter of St. John; verses 16-20 of the Twenty-eighth Chapter of St. Matthew.

LESSON CCXII.

TEXT.—"And after eight days, again His disciples were within: and Thomas with them. Jesus cometh the doors being shut, and stood in the midst, and said: Peace be to you. Then He saith to Thomas: Put in thy finger hither, and see My hands, and bring hither thy hand, and put it into My side: and be not faithless, but believing. Thomas answered, and said to Him: my Lord, and my God." (John xx. 26-28.)

REFLECTION.—Faith knows no doubt.

637. How long did Christ remain with the apostles?
He remained about forty days, during which He spoke

to them of the kingdom which He had come to establish. He explained His Gospel more fully to them, so that they might be able to preach it intelligently, and thus build the Church of God in the hearts of men. He spoke to them of the mission which they were to receive.

638. What authority did He give to them?

He gave to them authority over the whole world that they might do as He had done and share His power with Him. They had been constituted priests of His sacrifice, and were to offer for all time and in all places the holy sacrifice of His body and blood.

639. What was the teaching power which they were to possess?

It was a power to preach the Gospel of Christ to every creature, to evangelize the world and to convert the world to God. They were to teach what He taught them, and also such development of that teaching as the Holy Spirit of God would dictate, whom He was to send to them at Pentecost.

Primacy of St. Peter.

Read carefully and study verses 15-24 of the Twenty-first Chapter of St. John; verses 18-20 of the Ninth Chapter of St. Luke; verses 27-29 of the Eighth Chapter of St. Mark.

LESSON CCXIII.

TEXT.—" Going therefore teach ye all nations: baptizing them in the name of the Father, and of the Son, and of the Holy Ghost: Teaching them to observe all things whatsoever I have commanded you: and behold I am with you all days, even to the consummation of the world." (Matt. xxviii. 19, 20.)

REFLECTION.—Commission of the Church.

640. What was to be the sign of His faithful people?

They were to believe and be baptized and thus enter His

Church, which as the pillar and ground of truth was to show man true religion, and by its sacraments bring Christ's life into theirs, and thus save their souls.

641. What was the power of the keys?

It was the fulfilment of the promise made to the apostles when He told them that all power was His and that He would share that power with them, for He said to Peter: "I will give to thee the keys of the kingdom of heaven." This power of binding and loosing, of forgiving sin and retaining it, Christ gave to them after the Resurrection, when He said: "Whose sins you shall forgive they are forgiven them."

642. Is all that Christ did and said written in the gospels?

By no means, as we may see in St. John xxi. 25, where he says: "But there are also many other things which Jesus did; which, if they were written every one, the world itself, I think, would not be able to contain the books that should be written." The apostles were to make known all that they heard, and thus the world was to know the truth.

643. What authority did Christ give to Peter?

He gave the primacy to Peter, as we see in St. John xxi. 15–24, thus constituting him the prince of the apostolic college and the visible head of His Church. Peter was made the shepherd of the whole flock of Jesus Christ, of both lambs and sheep, and hence he was to be the infallible teacher in faith and morals, with supreme authority in the Church. All this was to pass to his successors, that thus the Church would always be to men as Christ Himself.

The Ascension.

Read verses 6–9 of the First Chapter of the Acts of the Apostles; also verses 50–53 of the Twenty-fourth Chapter of St. Luke.

LESSON CCXIV.

TEXT.—" And He led them out as far as Bethania: and lifting up His hands He blessed them. And it came to pass, whilst He blessed them, He departed from them, and was carried up to heaven. And they adoring went back into Jerusalem with great joy: and they were always in the Temple praising and blessing God. Amen." (Luke xxiv. 50–53.)

REFLECTION.—Heaven our home.

644. When did Christ ascend into heaven?

Christ ascended into heaven forty days after the Resurrection, after He had established His Church and instituted the sacraments, and taught His doctrines fully to the apostles.

645. Where did the Ascension take place?

It took place at Mount Olivet, to which Christ and His apostles came by way of Bethany. He ascended from the middle summit of the mount and within view of Jerusalem. Little by little the sacred body of Christ ascended, until it was lost to sight. The Ascension is said to have occurred about noon.

646. What became of the apostles after the Ascension?

They returned to Jerusalem with great joy, to await the fulfilment of Christ's last promise that He would send the Holy Ghost to teach them all truth, and abide with them forever.

" Many other signs also did Jesus in the sight of His disciples, which are not written in this book. But these are written that you may believe that Jesus is the Christ, the Son of God: and that believing you may have life in His name."—St. John xx. 30, 31.

BIBLE DICTIONARY.

A LIST OF BIBLICAL AND OTHER NAMES CONTAINED IN "NEW TESTAMENT STUDIES," WITH THEIR PRONUNCIATION AND DEFINITION.

Aaron (ăr'on), *enlightened*. The first high priest of the Jews, brother of Moses and Miriam.

Abia (ā-bī'a), *my father is God*. Descendant of Eleazar and chief of the eighth course in the divisions of the priests.

Alexandria (ăl'ĕx-ăn'dri-a). The Grecian capital of Egypt, founded by Alexander the Great, B.C. 332.

Allen, Cardinal (ăl'lĕn). A noted English cardinal who founded the English College at Douay in France in 1574.

Andrew (ăn'drụ), *manly*. One of the twelve apostles and the brother of Peter.

Angel (ān'jel). One of God's messengers.

Anna (ăn'na), *grace*. A prophetess who was in the Temple when Christ was presented to the Lord, by His parents.

Annas (ăn'nas). Father-in-law to Caiphas, and at one time a high priest.

Antioch (ăn'ti-ŏk). The capital of Syria, and the official residence of the Roman governors, on the Orontes River and near the Lebanon Range.

Antonia (ăn-tō'ni-a). A castle built by Herod, near the Temple of Jerusalem, and named after his friend Anthony.

Apocalypse (a-pŏk'a-lȳpse), *revelation*. The last book of the New Testament, and written by St. John as Revelations.

Arabia (a-rā'bi-a), *arid*. A large peninsula in the southwestern part of Asia between the Red Sea, the Indian Ocean, and the Persian gulf.

Aramaic (ăr'a-mā'ik). Name applied to the northern branch of the Semitic languages, including Syriac and Chaldaic.

Archelaus (ar'ke-lā'us), *ruler of the people.* Son of Herod the Great.

Arimathea (ăr'i-ma-thē'a), *heights.* A town in Judea, the home of Joseph who begged the body of Christ for burial.

Arimathea, Joseph of. A wealthy citizen, a member of the Sanhedrim, who became a disciple of Christ.

Ascalon (ăs'ka-lŏn). A seaport town ten miles north of Gaza. It was famous during the Crusades.

Ascension (ăs-sĕn'shun). The event which commemorates Christ's ascending into heaven in the presence of His apostles.

Aser (ā'ser). One of the twelve tribes of Israel, occupying the western portion of Galilee.

Assyrians (as-syr'i-ans). The people of Assyria, a great empire of western Asia, now known as Kurdistan.

Athanasius (ăth'a-nā'zhi-ŭs), *immortal.* One of the Greek Fathers of the Church, A.D. 296–373.

Augustine, St. (aw-gŭs'tĭn or aw'gŭs-tēn), *imperial.* Bishop of Hippo in Africa, a doctor of the Church, A.D. 354–430.

Azymes (ăz'ĭms), *unleavened.* The feast of the unleavened bread among the Jews.

Babylonia (băb'y̆-lō'ni-a), *babel* = "*confusion,*" or "*gate of God.*" The country of which Babylon was the capital, located in western Asia.

Baltimore, Council of. The council here referred to was held in Baltimore in 1884.

Barabbas (bar-ăb'bas), *son of Abba.* A noted criminal, chosen by the Jews in preference to Christ.

Bartholomew (bar-thŏl'o-mew), *a warlike son.* One of the apostles, and thought to be Nathanael.

Benedict XIV. (bĕn'e-dĭkt), *blessed.* A Roman Pontiff, A.D. 1675–1758.

Bethabara (bĕth-ăb'a-ra), *house of the ford.* Supposed to be on the side east of the Jordan, between the Dead Sea and the Sea of Galilee. It is thought that Jesus was baptized at this ford.

Bethany (bĕth'a-ny), *house of dates.* A village on the eastern slope of Mount Olivet.

Bethphage (bĕth'fāj), *house of green figs.* A town near Bethany.

Cæsar (cē'sar). A name applied to the Roman emperors.

Cæsar Augustus. Emperor of Rome from 27 B.C. to 14 A.D.

Caiphas (kā'i-făs), *depression.* The high priest at the time of the crucifixion. He was the son-in-law of Annas.

Calvary (kăl'va-ry), *skull*. The place where Our Lord was crucified, so called from its conical shape.

Cana (kā'na). A village in Galilee four or five miles northeast of Nazareth.

Canon (kăn'on). A rule or measure. Here it applies to the collection of sacred books.

Capharnaum (kă-phär'na-ŭm). A town in Galilee on the northwestern shore of the lake.

Caspar (kăs'par). According to Venerable Bede, this was the name of one of the Magi.

Cephas (cē'fas), *rock*. A Syriac name given to Simon Peter by Christ. In Latin it was *Petra*, or rock.

Cesarea (cĕs'a-rē'a). The chief Roman city of Palestine in New Testament times. It was on the Mediterranean.

Cesarea Philippi (cĕs'a-rē'a phĭ-lĭp'pī). A town at the base of Mount Hermon, where Peter made his great profession.

Chaldaic (kal-dā'ĭk). The language of the people of Chaldea.

Challoner, Rev. Richard (chăl'lon-er). An English priest and writer, who annotated the Douay Bible in 1758.

Cherubim (chĕr'ụ-bĭm). Winged figures used on the mercy-seat of the Ark in the Temple.

Chusa (kū'-za), *a seer*. The steward of Herod Antipas. His wife, Joanna, was one of the women who ministered to Christ.

Clement of Rome, St. (klĕm'ĕnt). Third successor of St. Peter as Pope, about A.D. 96.

Cleophas (klē'o-făs), *very renowned*. Supposed to be the same as Alpheus.

Cubit (kū'bĭt). A measure of length among the Jews, the distance from the elbow to the extremity of the middle finger, or about eighteen inches.

Cyprian, St. (sĭp'ri-an), *of Cyprus*. A Latin Father, bishop of Carthage, A.D. 200–258.

Cyrene, Simon of (cȳ-rē'ne). The man who was forced to carry Christ's cross to Calvary.

Damasus, St. (dăm'as-us). A Roman Pontiff who induced St. Jerome to translate the Bible.

David (dā'vĭd), *well beloved*. The greatest of all the kings who ruled Israel. He was born B.C. 1085 and ruled for forty years, from 1050 until 1010 B.C.

Decapolis (dĕ-căp'ō-lĭs), *ten cities.* A portion of Palestine mainly on the east side of the Jordan; it contained ten cities.

Deutero-canonical (deū'ter-o-kăn-ŏn'i-cal), *second canon.* Those books of the Bible about which some in the Church entertained doubts, before the General Council gave a decision.

Deuteronomy (deū'tĕr-ŏn'o-my), *the second law.* The fifth book of the Bible and the last of the Pentateuch.

Dismas (dĭs'mas). Supposed to be the name of the penitent thief.

Dives (dī'vēs). The rich man whom Christ spoke of in the parable.

Dominic, St. (dŏm'i-nĭk). The founder of the Order of Preachers known as Dominicans, 1170-1221.

Douay (doo'ā). A town in the north of France where an English translation of the Old Testament was published in 1610.

Edomite (ē'dom-īte), *red.* The inhabitants of Edom or Idumea, which was given as a birthright to Esau.

Egypt (ē'jўpt). The valley of the Nile in the northeastern part of Africa, the most famous country in ancient history.

Egyptian (ē'jўp'shŭn). Natives of Egypt or pertaining to Egypt.

Elders (ĕl'ders). A term used to designate the heads of tribes, or a tribunal chosen from the older people.

Elias (ĕ-lī'as) or Elijah, *Jehovah is my God.* One of the great prophets of the Old Testament.

Elizabeth (e-lĭz'a-bĕth), *God the oath.* The wife of Zachary and mother of St. John the Baptist.

Emmanuel (ĕm-măn'u-ĕl), *God with us.* One of the titles of Our Lord.

Ephesus (ĕph'e-sŭs). An important city of Asia Minor.

Esdrelon (es-drē'lon). The great plain of Galilee.

Eucharist (yū'ka-rĭst), *the giving of thanks.* The Sacrament of the body and blood of Christ.

Eugenius IV (yū-jē'ni-us). A Roman Pontiff, 1383-1447.

Evangelist (e-văn'je-lĭst), *messenger of good tidings.* A term applied to those who wrote the gospels.

Exegesis (ĕks'e-jē'sĭs). A critical explanation of the text of Scripture.

Florence, Council of (flŏr'ens). One of the great councils of the Church held in Florence, Italy, 1447.

Gabriel (gā'bri-el), *man of God.* Called the Angel of the Incarnation because he was specially charged with the message to Zachary and to the Blessed Virgin.

Galilee (găl'i-lē). The most northern of the provinces of Palestine at the time of Christ.

Galilee, Sea of. Named from the province of Galilee, twelve or fourteen miles long and six or seven miles wide.

Garizim (jăr'i-zĭm). A mountain in Ephrem near Sichem, from which blessings were pronounced. It was the site of the first Samaritan temple.

Genesareth (je-nĕs'a-rĕth). Same as the Sea of Galilee.

Genesis (jĕn'e-sĭs), *origin*. The first book of the Old Testament, so called because it is the history of creation.

Gentile (jĕn'tīle). Name given by the Jews to all who did not know the true God.

Gentiles, Court of the. The outer court of the Temple, where the uncircumcised could stand.

Gesmas (gĕs'mas). This is thought to be the name of the impenitent thief.

Gethsemani (gĕth-sĕm'a-nī), *oil-press*. A garden across the brook of Cedron, at the foot of Mount Olivet, where Christ had His agony.

Golgotha (gŏl'go-tha), *skull*. The Hebrew name of the place where Christ was crucified.

Greek (grēk). The language of the people of Greece.

Gregory the Great, St. (grĕg'o-ry). One of the great Popes who ruled the Church.

Hattin, Horns of (hăt'tĭn). So called because of the small cones on the ridge, which took its name from the village of Hattin near its base.

Hebrews (hē'brews), *descendants of Heber*. Name given to all the descendants of Jacob. They were called Israelites and also Jews.

Hebron (hē'brŏn), *friendship*. An ancient town in Palestine, about twenty miles south of Jerusalem.

Heli (hē'lī), *elevation*. The father of St. Joseph.

Hermon, Mount (hĕr'mŏn), *holy*, or "*the snowy top*." A high southern part of the mountains of Anti-Libanus, north of the Sea of Galilee.

Herod Antipater (ăn-tĭp'a-ter). Son of Herod the Great. After his father's death he ruled the tetrarchy of Galilee and Perea.

Herod the Great (hĕr'od). Second son of Antipater, the tyrant who massacred the Innocents. He was king of Judea B.C. 40.

Hillel (hĭl'lĕl), *praise.* This is thought to be the name of one of the doctors with whom Christ disputed in the Temple.

Hinnom (hĭn'nŏm). A valley to the south and west of Jerusalem. The term Gehenna (Ge Hinnom), hell, comes from this valley.

Hippo (hĭp'pō). A city in Africa, of which St. Augustine was bishop.

Holy of holies. The most sacred place in the Temple, where the Ark was placed.

Holy Place. This was outside the Holy of holies and separated from it by the veil of the Temple.

Holy Spirit. The Third Person of the Most Holy Trinity.

Homer (hō'mer). The great epic poet of Greece, who lived about 1000 years B.C.

Hosanna (hō-săn'na), *save, we beseech.* The cry of the Jews when they greeted Christ entering Jerusalem in triumph.

Incarnation (ĭn'kar-nā'shŭn). The mystery of the divine and human natures in one person in Christ.

Innocents (ĭn'nō-cĕnts). The children of Bethlehem put to death by order of Herod, in the hope that he might destroy the child Jesus.

Irenæus, St. (ĭr'ĕ-nē'us). A Greek bishop of Lyons in early ages.

Isaias (ī-zā'yas), *Jehovah's salvation.* The son of Amos and one of the great prophets.

Israel (ĭs'rā-ĕl), *the prince that prevails with God.* The surname of Jacob. It is also used to designate the whole race of Jacob's posterity.

Issachar (ĭs'sa-kär), *God hath given me my hire.* The fifth son of Jacob and Lia.

Itala (ĭt'a-la). An early Latin version of the Scriptures, called also the Italic Version.

Jacob, Well of (jā'kob), *supplanter.* A well in the territory purchased by Jacob.

Jairus (jā'i-rus), *whom Jehovah enlightens.* A ruler in the Jewish synagogue whose child was healed by Christ.

James (jāmes), *the supplanter.* One of the three favorite apostles; the brother of John and the son of Zebedee.

James the Lesser. One of the apostles, son of Alpheus and Mary.

Jeremias (jĕr'ĕ-mī'as), *whom Jehovah set up.* One of the four great prophets.

Jericho (jĕr'i-kō), *fragrance.* An ancient city in the valley of the Jordan about six miles north of the Dead Sea.

Jerome (jĕ-rōm'), *holy name.* One of the Latin Fathers, the translator of the Bible into Latin.

Jerusalem (jĕ-roo'sa-lĕm), *inheritance of peace.* The capital of Palestine, thirty-two miles from the Mediterranean and eighteen miles from the river Jordan.

Joachim (jō'a-kĭm), *the Lord will set up.* The father of the Blessed Virgin.

Job (jōb), *one persecuted.* A famous patriarch of Hus in Edom, of great piety. He lived before the time of Abraham.

John, *the grace of God,* **Boanērges** (bō'a-nēr'gēz), *son of thunder.* The beloved disciple, son of Zebedee and brother of James.

John the Baptist, *the grace or gift of Jehovah.* The son of Zachary and Elizabeth and the herald of Christ.

Jona (jō'na). The father of St. Peter, who was called Simon Bar-Jona.

Joppe (jŏp'pe), *beauty.* An ancient city on the Mediterranean, about thirty-five miles northwest of Jerusalem, now called Jaffa.

Jordan (jŏr'dan), *the descender.* The principal river in Palestine, 120 miles long, rising in Mount Hermon and emptying into the Dead Sea.

Joseph (jō'zef), *he will add.* The espoused husband of the Virgin Mary and foster-father of Christ; a carpenter of Nazareth.

Josue (jŏs'u-e), *whose help is Jehovah.* The son of Nun of the tribe of Ephraim, who became the successor of Moses.

Judas Iscariot (jū'das ĭs-kăr'i-ot). One of the twelve apostles; the one who betrayed Christ.

Judas or **Thaddeus** (thăd'dē-ŭs), *praise.* One of the apostles, a brother of James; called also Jude.

Judea (jū-dē'a). A province in Palestine, and applied to that part of Chanaan occupied by those who returned to Palestine after the captivity.

Judith (jū'dĭth), *Jewess.* A Jewish maiden who saved Bethulia from the tyrant Holofernes.

Latin (lăt'in). The language of the ancient Romans.

Levi (lē'vī), *crown.* The third son of Jacob and Lia, the head of one of the tribes of Israel.

Levites (lē'vītes). The descendants of Levi, who served the priests in the Temple.

Leviticus (le-vĭt'i-kŭs). The third book of the Old Testament, taking its name from its contents.

Lingard, Rev. John (lĭn'gard). An English priest who wrote the history of England.

Magi (mā'jī), (in Persian) *priests*. The wise men who came from the East to Bethlehem to do homage to the Saviour.

Malchus (măl'kŭs), *reigning*. The high priest's servant whose ear was cut off by Peter in the garden, when Jesus was apprehended.

Manna (măn'na), *what is this?* The food supplied by God to the Jews in the wilderness.

Mark (märk). One of the Evangelists, a disciple of St. Peter.

Mary Magdalen (măg'da-len). The sinful woman of Jerusalem who was converted by Christ.

Matthew (măth'thụ). *gift of God*. One of the twelve apostles; the writer of the first Gospel.

Mediterranean (mĕd'i-ter-rā'ne-an), *middle land*. The Great Sea, as it is called in Scripture, enclosed by Europe, Asia, and Africa.

Melcher (mĕl'ker). The name of one of the Magi who came to Bethlehem to adore Christ.

Merom (mē'rom), *high place*. The name of a lake in the north of Palestine, through which the Jordan runs.

Messias (mĕs sī'as), *Anointed One*. Term applied to Christ as the One sent by God for man's redemption.

Milner, Rev. John (mĭl'ner). A famous English priest who wrote a great work in defence of the Church.

Miracle (mĭr'a-kl), *wonder*. A supernatural event brought about in nature by the power of God.

Moses (mō'zez), *drawn out*. The great law-giver of the Jews, son of Amram and Jochabed of the tribe of Levi.

Mount of Beatitudes (be-ăt'i-tūdz). The mountain on which Christ sat when He gave the great sermon on the Beatitudes.

Naim (nā'im), *beauty*. A town in Galilee, now called Nein.

Nathanael (na-thăn'a-ĕl), *gift of God*. He was from Cana in Galilee—supposed to be the same as Bartholomew.

Nazarenes (năz'a-rēnes). Residents of Nazareth; also applied to followers of Jesus.

Nazareth (năz'a-rĕth), *separated.* A town in Galilee about sixty-six miles from Jerusalem.

Nazarite (năz'a-rīte), *to separate.* One bound by vow especially to total abstinence from wine and liquors.

Nabuzardan (năb'u-zăr'dăn), *Nebo sends prosperity.* A captain of the bodyguard of Nebuchadonosor, the great Babylonian king.

Nephthali (nĕf'tha-lī), *my wrestling.* The territory given to the tribe descended from Nephthali, the fifth son of Jacob.

Nicodemus (nĭk'o-dē'mus), *victory of the people.* A ruler of the Jews, a Pharisee, who sought Christ and became His follower.

Nimrim (nĭm'rim), *limpid.* A stream of water in the land of Moab.

Nisan (nī'san). Name of a Hebrew month, corresponding to our month of April.

Numbers, Book of (nŭm'bers). Fourth book of Moses, and so called because of the two censuses found recorded in it.

Olives, Mount of. Same as Mount Olivet.

Olivet, Mount (ŏl'i-vet). A noted mountain east of Jerusalem.

Orientals (o-ri-ĕnt'als). Natives of the Orient or East. Applied to Eastern Christians of the Greek rite.

Origen (ŏr'ĭ-jen). A Christian writer of Alexandria, A.D. 186–253.

Palestine (păl'es-tīn), *a land of sojourners.* The Holy Land, bounded on the north by Syria, on the east by the river Euphrates and the Great Desert, on the south by Negeb, and on the west by the Mediterranean.

Parable (păr'a-ble), *comparison.* Teaching by figures of speech.

Pasch (păsk). The feast of the Passover among the Jews—a term applied to Easter.

Passover (pass'ō-ver), *passing over.* The principal feast of the Jews, reminding them of the sparing of the families of the Israelites when the destroying angel killed the first-born of Egypt.

Patriarch (pā'tre-ärk), *father of families.* The head of each great family or tribe. It is also applied to the founder of the family.

Paul (paul), *little.* An apostle, a native of Tarsus in Cilicia, who was converted to the faith by a miracle.

Pennyworth (pĕn'ny-wŭrth). A Roman silver coin equivalent to about sixteen cents. A penny was a regular day's wages.

Pentateuch, The (pĕn'ta-tūk), *book divided into five parts.* The name given to the first five books of Moses, found at the beginning of the Old Testament.

Pentecost (pĕn'te-kŏst), *fiftieth.* A great feast among the Jews fifty days after the Passover, called *Feast of Weeks.* Also the day of the descent of the Holy Ghost upon the apostles, now a feast celebrated seven weeks after Easter.

Perea (pĕr-ē'a). A territory to the east of the Jordan between the Sea of Galilee and the Dead Sea.

Persia (pĕr'shi-a), *pure.* A country in central Asia.

Peter (pē'ter), *stone* or *rock.* The prince of the apostles.

Pharisees (phăr'i-sees), *separated.* A sect among the Jews.

Philip (phĭl'ip), *lover of horses.* An apostle of Bethsaida.

Phœnicia (fe-nish'Ia). A country north of Palestine between the Lebanon Mountains and the Mediterranean.

Pilate (pī'late). The sixth Roman procurator or governor of Judea.

Pope Pius VI. A Roman Pontiff, A.D. 1717–1799.

Pope Pius VII. A Roman Pontiff, A.D. 1742–1823.

Presentation (pres'en-tā'shŭn). The ceremony which the Jewish law required for every first-born male child forty days after birth.

Primacy (prī'ma-sȳ), *first.* It here refers to the Pope as the first principal or supreme bishop of the Christian Church.

Proto-Canonical (prō'tō-ka-nŏn'I-kl). Books of the First Canon.

Ptolemy (tŏl'e-mȳ). One of the Egyptian kings of the Greek dynasty.

Purification (pū'rĭ-fĭ-kā'shŭn). A Jewish ceremony by which a Jewish mother was declared cleansed.

Quarantania (kwŏr'an-tău'ya), *fortieth.* The mountain where it is said Christ permitted the great temptation.

Rabbi (răb'bī), *my master.* A title of respect given by the Jews to the doctors of the law.

Rachel (rā'chĕl), *a ewe.* The daughter of Laban, the wife of Jacob, and the mother of Joseph and Benjamin.

Rama (rā'mä), *high place.* A city of the tribe of Benjamin near Jerusalem.

Rheims (rēmz). A city of France where an English translation of the New Testament was made in 1582.

Ruth (rōōth), *friend* or *beauty*. A Moabite woman, the wife of Booz. Their son Obed was the father of Jesse, who was the father of David. Hence Ruth is mentioned in the genealogy of Christ.

Sadducees (săd'du-ceez). A religious sect among the Jews.

Safed (sa-fĕd'). A city on a hill, seen from the mount on which Christ gave His discourse.

Samaria (sa-mā'ri-a or săm'a-rī'a), *watch-post*. The central province of Palestine, south of Galilee and north of Judea.

Samaritan (sa-mărī-tan). A native of Samaria.

Samuel (săm'u-el), *heard of God*. A celebrated Hebrew prophet, and the last one of the judges of Israel.

Sanhedrim (săn'hĕ-drĭm), *with seats*. The great council of the Jews.

Scribes (skrībs') *writers*. Writers among the Jews, copyists and expounders of the law.

Septuagint (sĕp'tu-a-jĭnt), *seventy*. The name given to the Greek version of the Old Testament, because it was believed to be the work of seventy-two translators.

Sichem (sī'kĕm), *shoulder*. A town in the valley between Mounts Hebal and Garizim, called also Shechem.

Simeon (sĭm'e-on), *obedient*. A pious old man inspired by God to meet the parents of Jesus in the Temple, to take the Saviour in his arms and predict remarkable things of Him.

Simon Peter (sī'mon pē'ter). The chief of the apostles, whose name was Simon, afterwards changed to Peter.

Sinai (sī'naī), *burning bush*. The mountain on which Moses received the Law.

Solomon (sŏl-o-mon), *peaceful*. A king of Israel, the son and successor of David, and called the wisest of men.

Synagogue (sĭn'a-gŏg), *assembly*. Meeting-place of the Jews.

Synoptic (sĭn-ŏp'tĭk), *with view*. A general view of the whole gospel, or the principal parts of it.

Syria (syr'i-a). At the time of Christ it was a Roman province.

Temple (tĕm'ple). The chief place of worship among the Jews, erected upon Mount Moria, in Jerusalem.

Thabor (tā'bor), *height*. A mountain of Palestine, on which Christ was transfigured.

Theophilus (thē-ŏf'ĭ-lŭs), *lover of God.* A distinguished person to whom St. Luke addressed both his gospel and his book of the Acts of the Apostles.

Thomas (tŏm'as), *a twin.* One of the twelve apostles, called also Didymus.

Tiberius (tī-bē'ri-ŭs). A Roman emperor, the stepson and successor of Augustus, B.C. 42 to A.D. 37.

Torah (tō'ra). The Book of the Law among the Jews.

Toulouse, Council of (too'looz). A city in France where a council of the Church was held in 1229.

Transfiguration (trăns-fĭg'u-rā'shŭn). A miracle in the life of Christ which took place probably on the southern slope of Mount Hermon or on Mount Thabor.

Trent (trĕnt). A city in the Austrian Tyrol where one of the greatest councils of the Church was held, A.D. 1545–1563.

Virgin Mary (vĕr'jin mā'ry), *green, bitter.* The name given to the Mother of Our Saviour.

Vulgate (vŭl'gāt), *common, current text.* Name given to the Latin version of the Scriptures, because of its common use in the Latin Church.

Zabulon (zăb'u-lŏn), *a habitation.* The sixth son of Jacob and Lia; also the name of one of the twelve tribes of Israel.

Zachary (zăk'a-rў), *remembered by Jehovah.* The husband of Elizabeth and the father of John the Baptist.

Zacheus (zăk-kē-us), *pure.* A rich Jew resident of Jericho, and a tax collector, with whom Christ spent a day.

Zebedee (zĕb'e-dee), *Jehovah's gift.* The husband of Salome and father of the apostles James the Greater and John.

Zion, Mount of (zī'on or sī-on), *dry, sunny mount.* The southwestern hill of Jerusalem.

www.ingramcontent.com/pod-product-compliance
Lightning Source LLC
Chambersburg PA
CBHW031744230426
43669CB00007B/480